Help!
I'm Leading a
Children's Sermon

Volume Two:
Lent to
Pentecost

by marcia
taylor thompson

SMYTH&HELWYS
PUBLISHING, INCORPORATED · MACON, GEORGIA

M000004363

Smyth & Helwys Publishing, Inc.
6316 Peake Road
Macon, Georgia 31210-3960
1-800-747-3016
©2004 by Smyth & Helwys Publishing

Help! I'm Leading a Children's Sermon: Volume 2

The paper used in this publication meets the minimum requirements of
American National Standard for Information Sciences—
Permanence of Paper for Printed Library Materials.
ANSI Z39.48–1984. (alk. paper)

Library of Congress Cataloging-in-Publication Data

Thompson, Marcia Taylor, 1963-
Help! I'm leading a children's sermon : ready-to-use,
follows the Christian year, over 70 sermons
by Marcia Taylor Thompson.
p. cm.
ISBN 1-57312-331-5
1. Bible—Children's sermons.
2. Church year sermons.
3. Sermons, American—21st century.
I. Title.
BS491.5 .T48 2003
252'.53—dc21

2002153758

Table of Contents

Common Lectionary Year C

Appendix

Preface

See what love the Father has given us, that we should be called the children of God; and that is what we are. The reason the world does not know us is that it did not know him. Beloved, we are God's children now; what we will be has not yet been revealed. What we do know is this: when he is revealed, we will be like him, for we will see him as he is. And all who have this hope in him purify themselves, just as he is pure. (1 John 3:1-3)

The season of Lent and the celebration of Easter offer a time to reflect on God's love for us. As the writer of 1 John says, we are children of God now. We resemble God now and will resemble God even more when God's kingdom is completed. Lent is an opportunity to lead children to ask, "How much do we resemble God?" We can guide children, and ourselves, through Scripture and prayer to dig deep within for a fuller understanding of what it means to resemble God.

Easter is a time to celebrate God's love shown to us in Christ. It is an opportunity to celebrate the love and hope expressed in the resurrection. During this season, we may lead children and ourselves to a deeper understanding of purity and holiness—living in the likeness of Christ. We express joy and thanksgiving for God's great gift. Easter is the reason we gather each week to worship.

This book contains a collection of children's sermons based on the Common Lectionary Years A, B, and C from Lent through Pentecost. A handy index of subjects covered is provided in the back for use in churches which do not follow the lectionary. Another index of Scripture covered is provided for tying the children's sermon to particular passages. The sermons are intended to involve children creatively in worship and proclamation of the Word. You will find two sermons for each Sunday. Each emphasizes Scripture and includes a key verse(s) to be read within the sermon. Many of the sermons present opportunities to tell the complete story to the children. The goal of this book is to help you invite children to participate in corporate worship in a meaningful way. You do this by telling stories, guiding dramatic participation, asking questions, showing visual props, and using hands-on activities to explain scriptural themes and/or stories.

The introduction to each sermon lists the liturgical date, the Scripture, a key verse or verses, key concepts, and the preparation and materials you will need for your time with the children. By including key verses or complete narratives, I hope that those who share God's Word with children will use the Bible as a visible presence so children will understand its importance and know that we share God's message with them. Written in conversational language, the sermons cover every Sunday of each lectionary year. An appendix includes Sundays in the Lent and Easter seasons that are the same for all three cycles.

This book is a guide to help you create your own children's sermons. Each person has a unique style and personality that will shape the delivery. Use the sermons as a beginning point and adjust them, using personal stories that you think will be meaningful for the children in your church. Take time to study the Scripture passages just as you would for any proclamation of God's Word. Pray for guidance as you prepare, seeking to share the story or message God wants you to share. Pray for the children who will hear your words.

As you prepare, make sure the children's sermon fits within the larger context of worship. Do not use the children's sermon as gap filler. It is an element of worship that needs to be given as much thought as the music, pastor's sermon, and prayers. All elements of worship should set the tone and focus the direction of the service. All elements should lead the worshiper to God and God to the worshiper. Children are being spiritually formed through worship, and we are called to provide meaningful ways for them to understand why we do what we do each time we gather. Included within this set of sermons are explanations of various elements of worship.

As you prepare, practice the sermons. The more comfortable you are with the message, the more relaxed you will be with the children. Some people are gifted at being with children, while others have to work at it. As you involve the children in the sermon, be aware of the risks. Be ready for the unexpected. Often the most involved, risky sermons provide a lively proclamation of God's Word that is real for the children (and the rest of the congregation).

As you worship during the seasons of Lent and Easter, use this time with the children to involve them fully within the life of the church. Let them show you and the congregation how they resemble God as you share with them. Invite the children and their families to the discipline of Scripture reading and prayer. Model for them and call them to a life of holiness together. Take this opportunity to share the good news of Jesus Christ with the children, knowing that through his love and grace we can gain deeper understanding of purity and holiness—living in the likeness of Christ.

Common Lectionary
Year A

Talking Snakes

Date: First Sunday in Lent

Scripture: Genesis 2:15-17; 3:1-7

Key Verse: Now the serpent was more crafty than any other wild animal that the Lord God had made. He said to the woman, "Did God say, 'You shall not eat from any tree in the garden'?" (Genesis 3:1)

Key Concept: Listening to God

Materials: Bible, real nonpoisonous snake or toy snake (optional)

Preparation: If someone in your church has a small, nonpoisonous pet snake, consider asking him or her to sit with the snake as you talk with the children. Otherwise, consider showing a toy snake.

[Person's name] has brought his/her pet snake for us to see. *(Let the pet's owner share information about his/her snake.)* Snakes look slimy, but when you feel them they're dry and smooth. Snakes grow fast, but their skin doesn't stretch so they get rid of their old skin. A new skin lies beneath the old one.

Snakes can be tricky. Some snakes hide from other animals by blending in with the trees or the ground. A parrot snake opens its mouth wide and tries to look scary. A milk snake is harmless, but it looks like a coral snake, so other animals are afraid of it. A grass snake tries to trick its enemies by playing dead. Snakes are some of God's amazing creatures.

Our story from Genesis is about a snake that talks to Eve. *(Open Bible.)* This is what it says in Genesis 3:1: *Now the serpent was more crafty than any other wild animal that the LORD God had made. He said to the woman, "Did God say, 'You shall not eat from any tree in the garden'?"*

What would it be like for a snake to talk to you? *(Let the children answer.)* Eve listened to the snake and did what God told her and Adam not to do. Why do you think Eve listened to the snake? *(Let the children respond with their ideas. Accept their answers as possible reasons.)*

Eve knew God had told them not to eat from a certain tree. The snake tricked her, and Eve listened to him. Eve didn't think about how she was being selfish. Sometimes that happens to us. We stop listening to God. We become selfish and try to get what we want. We do things God doesn't want us to do. But God still loves us and wants us to come back.

Do you know what the season of Lent is? It is a time to get ready to celebrate Easter. Why do we celebrate Easter? We remember that Jesus rose from the dead. One way to get ready for Easter is to think about things we do when we don't listen to God. Maybe we sin against God when we don't listen to our parents. Maybe we treat our friends in an unkind way. We ask God to forgive us for the wrong things we do. We ask God to help us listen to God instead of people who try to get us to do wrong.

A Time of Confession

Date: First Sunday in Lent

Scripture: Psalm 32

Key Verse: Then I acknowledged my sin to you, and I did not hide my iniquity; I said, "I will confess my transgressions to the Lord," and you forgave me the guilt of my sin. (Psalm 32:5)

Key Concepts: Prayer of confession, Lent

Materials: Bible, bulletin (Provide a bulletin if you print a prayer of confession to be read in unison. This can be adapted if you do not have a specific prayer of confession.)

Today is the first Sunday in Lent. Lent is a season of our church year that takes place for forty days before Easter. It doesn't include Sundays. During Lent we repent to get ready for Easter. When we repent, we feel sorry for our sins and stop doing them. Sin is not following God's way. It can be wrong thoughts, wrong words, or wrong actions.

(Open Bible.) In Psalm 32:5, the psalmist tells his sins to God. He uses big words like iniquity and transgressions, but they are other words that mean sin. The psalmist writes, *Then I acknowledged my sin to you, and I did not hide my iniquity; I said, "I will confess my transgressions to the LORD," and you forgave me the guilt of my sin.* He was sorry for turning away from God. He asked God to forgive and knew God forgave.

Each week, all of us come to worship together. A part of our worship is the prayer of confession. Together, we ask God to forgive us for our words, thoughts, or actions that didn't please God. It's a way we can tell God we are sorry for our sins and that we will try our best to stop doing them. Just like the psalmist, we know God forgives us. *(Depending on your tradition, you may want to elaborate on how we know God forgives us, the assurance of pardon, etc.)*

During Lent, we give special attention to repentance. Lent is a time when we all think about how we follow or don't follow God's way. We can learn more about what it means to be a Christian. Take this time before Easter with your family to pray and read Scripture so that you can know the right words, the right thoughts, and the right actions that are holy.

A New Home

Date: Second Sunday in Lent

Scripture: Genesis 12:1-4a

Key Verse: So Abram went, as the Lord had told him. Genesis 12:4a

Key Concept: Trust

Materials: Bible; suitcase packed with clothes, books, toys, other items

I brought my suitcase with me. Let's look inside and see what we might pack if we were going on a long trip. *(Open the suitcase and show the items you packed—i.e., clothes, snack food, toiletry items, entertainment, etc.)*

How would I pack if I were going to move and live somewhere else? *(Let the children answer. If any of the children have moved from one house to another, let them tell about what it was like.)* When you move, you take all the stuff in your house or apartment and move it to another house or apartment. It takes a lot of work to get everything ready. The grownups make plans. Sometimes you move because your mother or father got a job somewhere else. There is a reason to go to your new place to live. *(If any of the children have moved for a particular reason, mention them at this time. For example, "John moved because his dad got a job at the hospital here in town.")*

In our Old Testament lesson from Genesis 12, God asks someone to move. Do you know whom God asked to move? *(Give the children a chance to respond.)* It was Abram. He was later called Abraham. God told Abram to leave his country and go to a new place God would show him. Abram didn't know where that would be. He did what God told him to do because he trusted God. *(Open Bible.)* Genesis 12:4a says, *So Abram went, as the* LORD *had told him.* How do you think Abram felt not knowing where he was going? Do you think Abram trusted God when he left his family and went into the desert? *(Let the children respond.)*

When we trust, it means we believe God cares for us and will help us in everything we do. We know this is true because God loves us.

No Sleep

Date: Second Sunday in Lent

Scripture: Psalm 121

Key Verses: He who keeps Israel will neither slumber nor sleep. The Lord is your keeper. (Psalm 121:4-5a)

Key Concept: God's care

Materials: Bible

What would it be like if you had to stay awake all night? *(Let the children respond. Expect a variety of answers.)* Do you think you could stay awake for one, two, or three nights in a row? *(Again let the children respond and talk with them according to their responses.)* Maybe I could stay awake for one night, but I know I couldn't stay awake two or three nights in a row. I would be cranky! I need to sleep. I bet you need to sleep too. In fact, I know you need to sleep. Sleep helps you grow. Your body uses a lot of energy as you play during the day, but it also uses energy to grow. We all get tired and we all need sleep.

Did you know there is someone who never sleeps? *(Let the children answer.)* God doesn't sleep. God is everywhere. God cares for people and creation all the time—every year, every month, every hour, every minute, every second. *(Open Bible.)* The psalmist who wrote Psalm 121 knew this: *He who keeps Israel will neither slumber nor sleep. The LORD is your keeper.* The psalmist wrote about how God cared for and protected God's people. God's people were sometimes called Israel. The psalmist said God was their keeper or their protector. God kept them safe and always watched, cared for, and protected them.

It's good to know God cares for us and protects us. God wants what is best for us. We can be sure God is our keeper. We are God's people and God is always watching, protecting, and caring for us too.

We Want It Now!

Date: *Third Sunday in Lent*

Scripture: *Exodus 17:1-7*

Key Verse: *"I will be standing there in front of you on the rock at Horeb. Strike the rock, and water will come out of it, so that the people may drink." Moses did so, in the sight of the elders of Israel. (Exodus 17:6)*

Key Concept: *Trusting God*

Materials: *Bible, large rock, stick*

Have you ever been in a store and seen something you wanted, but your parents wouldn't let you have it? *(Let the children respond.)* Sometimes we want things right now. I know I've felt that way before. We think we should have what we want when we want it.

(Open Bible.) Our story from Exodus is like this. Remember the story of baby Moses? When Moses grew up, God chose him to lead God's people out of Egypt to the promised land. The promised land would be a beautiful place with lots of food and drink. God's people didn't always do what God wanted them to do. They complained. They said, "We want water now" or "We want food now."

God's people had been walking and living in the desert. Moses led them. God's people got mad because they didn't have water. They scared Moses. He thought they would hurt him. Moses cried out to God in prayer. He asked God what to do with the people because they always complained and didn't trust God. God answered Moses and said, *"I will be standing there in front of you on the rock at Horeb. Strike the rock, and water will come out of it, so that the people may drink." Moses did so, in the sight of the elders of Israel. (Have Moses strike the rock with the stick.)* God provided the people with the water. They drank all they needed. God's people had complained and wanted proof that God was God. They didn't have much trust. *(Have the children join you again and thank them for their help.)*

What can we learn from this story? *(Expect a variety of answers. Reflect back the answers the children give.)* God wants us to believe and trust that God will provide. We can ask God through prayer for what we need, but we should not demand what we want.

God Bragging

Date: Third Sunday in Lent

Scripture: Romans 5:1-11

Key Verse: But more than that, we even boast in God through our Lord Jesus Christ. (Romans 5:11a)

Key Concept: Proclaiming God/Jesus

Materials: Bible

Have you ever heard anyone brag? What would person say if he or she bragged about being good at sports? *(Let the children answer. Guide the children not to include names in their stories.)* A girl or boy might say, "I'm better at basketball than you are." Or they might say, "I can jump higher than you can." When boys or girls say they are better at something, whether it's true or not, we call it bragging. When people brag, they think they are better than another person. Sometimes bragging hurts other people's feelings.

Another word for bragging is boasting. What would you say if I told you one thing that each of you could boast or brag about? Do you want to know? You can boast in God. *(Open Bible.)* Paul writes in Romans 5:11, *But more than that, we even boast in God through our Lord Jesus Christ.* Paul told the Christians in Rome that we can boast about our life in Jesus. This kind of boasting doesn't put one person above another person. This kind of boasting or bragging is telling the promises of Jesus that we know are certain. It's telling others through our words and our actions that we are followers of Jesus.

What are some ways we can brag about Jesus? What promises do we know are true? *(Let the children respond. Reflect back their answers so others can hear.)* We know Jesus loves us. We can brag about Jesus' love by loving others. There are so many ways we can brag about Jesus. I hope this week you will try to brag about Jesus in all you do and say.

It's Not What You Look Like

Date: **Fourth Sunday in Lent**

Scripture: **1 Samuel 16:1-13**

Key Verse: **But the Lord said to Samuel, "Do not look on his appearance or on the height of his stature, because I have rejected him; for the Lord does not see as [people] see; they look on the outward appearance, but the Lord looks on the heart." (1 Samuel 16:7)**

Key Concept: **Judging**

Materials: **Bible**

Preparation: **The first paragraph offers my personal example of something unattractive on the outside but beautiful within. Consider bringing your own example to show.**

I want to tell you about a time when I lived in Atlanta. When I drove to the store, I passed a group of apartments. They didn't look nice on the outside. *(Show a picture.)* They were built a long time ago. I didn't want to live there.

Soon, I needed an apartment that had more space. I looked at the different apartment buildings in the city. Someone told me about the apartments I saw on my way to the store. They told me if I looked on the inside, I would be surprised at how nice they were. I made an appointment to look at the apartments. When I went inside, I was amazed. They were beautiful on the inside! They were nicer than the apartment I lived in for two years. I had judged the apartments by what they looked like on the outside. I thought if they looked bad on the outside, then the inside would probably look bad too.

Samuel had the same problem when he went to find the person who would be the next king of Israel. Samuel thought he found someone to be the next king. *(Open Bible.)* In 1 Samuel 16:7, it says, *But the LORD said to Samuel, "Do not look on his appearance or on the height of his stature, because I have rejected him; for the LORD does not see as [people] see; they look on the outward appearance, but the LORD looks on the heart."*

Samuel saw all the sons of Jesse except for David. None of these sons was to be the king. David, the youngest son, was out with the sheep. God knew David was the one who would make a good king. Even though he was small and didn't look like a king, God said he would be the king of Israel. David loved God and tried to follow God's way. God knew David on the inside.

Sometimes we look at people from the outside without learning about who they are. They may look different from us or from most of our friends. We make judgments about people before we learn about them. When we judge people on the outside, we never find out what color they like, what games they like to play, what their family is like, and all sorts of things that make each person special. The people we meet could be great friends, good listeners, or fun pals. We need to try to get to know others instead of judging them for how they look. Then we have the chance to find the beauty God created in each of us. God thinks we are all beautiful and special because God made us.

Hide and Seek

Date: Fourth Sunday in Lent

Scripture: Ephesians 5:8-14

Key Verse: Try to find out what is pleasing to the Lord. (Ephesians 5:10)

Key Concept: Pleasing Jesus

Materials: Bible, small objects to hide, a list of the objects, marker

Preparation: Hide a few objects (three or four) around the front of the church. Be sure they are fairly easy to find. Make a list of the objects so the children will know what to look for and when they have found all items. Create a picture list for younger children. If the group is large, consider choosing one child at a time to search for an object.

I have hidden the objects written/drawn on this list. Can you find them for me? *(Allow time for the children to find the objects. Let them return to the group and continue.)* Was it hard to find these objects? *(Let the children answer.)* Do you think it would have been harder to find the objects if I had not told you what to look for? *(Let the children respond.)* Having a list makes it easier to search.

(Open Bible.) In Ephesians 5:10, Paul writes, *Try to find out what is pleasing to the Lord.* Paul asked the Christians in Rome to look for what Jesus wants them to do. Just like we played the game to find the objects, Paul tells us to find and do things that please Jesus. How can we find out how to please Jesus? *(Let the children respond. They may include reading the Bible, Sunday school teachers who help them learn, parents, friends, prayer, etc. Reflect back their answers and include others.)*

There are so many ways to find out what pleases Jesus. They aren't really hidden from us, but sometimes it seems that way. Our lives are busy. We must take time to try to find out what pleases Jesus. Remember to talk to your Sunday school teachers and parents, read the Bible, and pray. These are all ways to learn what pleases Jesus.

My Hero

Date: **Fifth Sunday in Lent**

Scripture: **Psalm 130**

Key Verse: **But there is forgiveness with you, so that you may be revered. (Psalm 130:4)**

Key Concept: **Reverence**

Materials: **Bible, superhero figure (positive role model)**

I brought a superhero figure today. Does anyone know who this is? *(Let the children tell what they know about the figure. If they are unfamiliar with the hero, talk about other heroes and what they do to help people. Choose positive superheroes the children will likely know.)*

A superhero is someone who is not real. Superheroes are make-believe. What is a real hero like? *(Let the children respond. Offer suggestions as necessary.)* A real hero is someone we respect. The person may have done something important to help others. We admire these heroes and sometimes want to be like them.

My greatest hero is God. I respect God. I admire God. I worship God. I want to be like God and do things to help others. God is a great hero. The psalmist knew this too. *(Open Bible.)* In Psalm 130:4, the psalmist writes, *But there is forgiveness with you, so that you may be revered.* When someone reveres us, they respect and admire us. God's gift of forgiveness was so great that the psalmist revered God.

Reverence is another form of the word revere. It means respect, follow, value, admire, worship, devotion, loyalty, attachment, awe, wonder, adoration, and love. *(Consider pausing after each word and talking about ways to show that particular trait.)* Reverence is honoring God. God is our greatest hero.

Full of Feeling

Date: Fifth Sunday in Lent

Scripture: John 11:1-45

Key Verses: When Jesus saw her weeping, and the Jews who came with her also weeping, he was greatly disturbed in spirit and deeply moved. . . . Jesus began to weep. (John 11:33, 35)

Key Concepts: Jesus' humanity, death, and feelings

Materials: Bible, children's book The Tenth Good Thing about Barney **by Judy Voirst**

(Begin by reading The Tenth Good Thing about Barney, *or have the children discuss the death of a pet or a loved one. If you choose the second option, be aware that that children have a variety of views about what actually happens when someone dies.)*

What feelings do we have when a pet dies or when a person we love dies? *(Let the children respond and reflect their answers back. If you read the book, you might want to use guiding questions about the characters and how they felt.)*

Did you know that Jesus had those feelings too? *(Open Bible.)* John 11 is the story about when Lazarus died. Lazarus had two sisters, Mary and Martha. They were sad that Lazarus had died. As Jesus walked near their house to visit them, Mary came to find him. She was upset and sad about the death of her brother. John 11:33, 35 says, *When Jesus saw her weeping, and the Jews who came with her also weeping, he was greatly disturbed in spirit and deeply moved. . . . Jesus began to weep.* Jesus was sad because his friend Mary was sad. Jesus was sad because Lazarus was his friend, too.

We don't often think of Jesus' feelings. Jesus was human and had feelings just like we do. Jesus knows what it's like to feel sad, happy, surprised, angry, upset, hurt, and all the other feelings we sometimes have. We know Jesus understands how we feel. We can talk to him through prayer because he knows what it's like to be human. He knows what it's like to be a child. He knows what it's like to be a grownup. *(Some of the children may know the end of the story. Be prepared to tell about Jesus' raising Lazarus from the dead if necessary.)*

Who Am I?

Date: Sixth Sunday in Lent (Palm Sunday)

Scripture: Matthew 21:1-11

Key Verses: When he entered Jerusalem, the whole city was in turmoil, asking, "Who is this?" The crowds were saying, "This is the prophet Jesus from Nazareth in Galilee." (Matthew 21:10-11)

Key Concepts: Jesus as God's Son/Savior

Materials: Bible

We're going to play a game called "Who Am I?" Listen to the sentences and see if you can guess the character I am describing. Raise your hand and I'll call on you.

Suggestions (or you can make up your own):
(1) I'm big and purple and I sing. I'm a dinosaur on public TV. Who am I? (Barney)
(2) I live in a pineapple on the bottom of the sea. I'm yellow and square and silly as can be. Who am I? (SpongeBob SquarePants)
(3) I live on Sesame Street. I have red fur from my head to my feet. Who am I? (Elmo)

You did a great job in our guessing game. A long time ago, on what we now call Palm Sunday, Jesus made his way into Jerusalem. It was a big parade with people running and shouting. Some people didn't know who Jesus was. *(Open Bible.)* Matthew 21:10-11, *When he entered Jerusalem, the whole city was in turmoil asking, "Who is this?" The crowds were saying, "This is the prophet Jesus from Nazareth in Galilee."*

The crowd was trying to find out who Jesus was. The people who had followed him into town said he was a prophet. Did anyone know who Jesus was? Some of them didn't know, so they asked. Others said he was a prophet. We know Jesus was God's Son. We know Jesus is our Savior—one who saved us from our sins. As we prepare for Easter, think about who Jesus is. Think about what Jesus did in the stories you know from the Bible. Then if friends ask you who Jesus is, you can tell them that he is God's Son and one who saved us from our sins.

Easter Life

Date: Easter Sunday

Scripture: Colossians 3:1-4

Key Verse: Set your minds on things that are above, not on things that are on earth. (Colossians 3:2)

Key Concept: Discipleship

Materials: Bible, WWJD bracelets or pencils to give to the children

Sometimes we read verses in our Bible that are hard to understand. The key verse for today might be hard for you to understand, so we will talk about what it means. *(Open Bible.)* Colossians 3:2 says, *Set your minds on things that are above, not on things that are on earth.* What do you think Paul meant when he said "things that are on earth"? *(Let the children respond. Guide them if necessary. Ask them what things are on earth. They will likely mention material things.)* What do you think Paul meant when he said think about "things that are above"? *(Let the children answer. Guide them as necessary. They may mention heaven.)*

Paul wrote these instructions for the church. He wanted to help Jesus by teaching people how to follow Jesus or how to be disciples. When Paul said to think about things that are above, he wanted us to think about Jesus and the way Jesus lived, talked, played, and worked. Paul told people not to think about things that are on earth. He didn't mean everything that was on earth, like *[name the items the children mentioned earlier]*. Paul meant that we should live, act, talk, play, and work in a way that pleases Jesus. Some of the things Paul included as earthly things were greed, anger, meanness, bad language, and lying. We don't need to focus on earthly things that are hurtful to us and to other people.

On this special Easter day, we can celebrate being followers of Jesus. We can remember how he loved people and always wanted what was best for them. If we are Jesus' followers or disciples, then we should want the best for others too. I have something that can help you remember to think of Jesus. It's a WWJD. WWJD means "What would Jesus do?" When you have this with you, remember to think about Jesus as you work at school, play with friends, talk, and in everything you do. This way, you can be Jesus' disciple and show others his love.

Occupied by God

Date: Second Sunday of Easter

Scripture: Psalm 16

Key Verse: I keep the Lord always before me; because he is at my right hand, I shall not be moved. (Psalm 16:8)

Key Concept: God's presence

Materials: Bible

Let's talk about the word "occupy." Do you know what it means? *(Let the children answer.)* Here is an example: I occupy the house that is on *(give your street address)*. That means I live in the house on that street. To occupy something means to live in something or to be in or on something. For example, I occupy this stool when I sit on it. I'm on the stool. You occupy the floor because you are sitting on it.

What would you say if I told you that I was occupied by God? It means God is with me all the time. Sometimes we might say God's Spirit lives inside us. That's what the psalmist meant in Psalm 16:8: *I keep the LORD always before me; because he is at my right hand I shall not be moved.* The psalmist knew that no matter what happened, God was always there. The psalmist prayed and worshiped God, thought about God all the time, and knew God was there to help every minute of every day.

That's true for us too. God is with us every minute of every day. Can any of you tell about a time when you knew God was with you? *(Let the children answer. Offer your own example.)* Just as the psalmist, we know God is everywhere. God is with us all the time. That's a special gift that no one else can give us.

O How I Love Jesus

Date: Second Sunday of Easter

Scripture: 1 Peter 1:3-9

Key Verse: Although you have not seen him, you love him; and even though you do not see him now, you believe in him and rejoice with an indescribable and glorious joy . . . . (1 Peter 1:8)

Key Concepts: Faith/Love

Materials: Bible; song; letters J, O, Y written vertically; marker

I have written a word on this piece of paper. *(Show the children the paper with the word "JOY" written in vertical capital letters.)* Can anyone read this word? *(Let a child answer.)* Last Sunday, we began our celebration of Easter. We will celebrate the Easter season for seven more weeks. Easter is a season of joy. When we have joy, we are glad and we celebrate our gladness. One of the ways we can have joy and celebrate gladness is to think of Jesus first. *(Write "esus" beside the "J" on your paper.)* Another way to celebrate the joy of Easter is to think of others before you think of yourself. *(Write "thers" beside "O" and "ourself" by "Y.")* This means we try not to be selfish. Being unselfish is sometimes hard, but we can always try.

In his letter, Peter talked about the joy we have through Jesus. *(Open Bible.)* In 1 Peter 1:8 he wrote, *Although you have not seen him, you love him; and even though you do not see him now, you believe in him and rejoice with an indescribable and glorious joy . . . .* Peter wrote to Christians who had not seen Jesus when he was human and lived in Bible lands. He wrote about the people's faith, what they believed without seeing. He wrote about their love and belief in Jesus that gave them great joy and gladness. It was so great, he could not describe it with words.

We can't see Jesus like people did when he lived as a man on earth more than 2,000 years ago. Still, we love and believe in Jesus. We believe because the story is in our Bible for us to read and because our parents and teachers have told us those stories of Jesus and his love for us. As you get older, your love and belief will grow, and you will continue to know joy and gladness because of Jesus.

Loving God

Date: *Third Sunday of Easter*

Scripture: *Psalm 116:1-4, 12-19*

Key Verse: *I love the Lord, because he has heard my voice and my supplications. (Psalm 116:1)*

Key Concept: *God's sovereignty*

Materials: *Bible, heart shape cut from red art paper*

What do you think of when you see this shape? *(Let the children answer.)* People use symbols to stand for other things. Today, I'm using this heart to stand for love. When you really love someone, how do you treat that person? *(Let the children respond. Reflect back the answers they give. Adapt the next part of the sermon based on what the children say.)*

When you really love someone, you try to be kind to the person. You do things together that you enjoy. You say nice things about the person you love. This doesn't mean you never have arguments or disagree. But even if you do have disagreements, you talk about them and still love each other. When we love someone, we want the best for that person.

(Open Bible.) In Psalm 116:1 the psalmist writes, *I love the Lord, because he has heard my voice and my supplications.* The psalmist believed God was sovereign. Sovereign means God is the one who is in charge of everything everywhere. The psalmist had deep love and trust for God. The psalmist knew God would listen, no matter what. Just like the psalmist, we can know that God loves us because God is in charge of everything everywhere.

The psalmist also followed God's commandments. In Jewish custom, to love God who was in charge of everything everywhere was to follow God's commandments. The psalmist showed the greatest love and respect to God by doing what God wanted. God told the people how to live through the Ten Commandments, and the psalmist knew this.

We can show God great love and respect. We can trust God and know that God loves us. We can love God by knowing and acting like God is in charge of everything everywhere and following God's commandments to love God and each other.

How Do We Know Jesus?

Date: Third Sunday of Easter

Scripture: Luke 24:13-35

Key Verse: Then beginning with Moses and all the prophets, he [Jesus] interpreted to them the things about himself in all the scriptures. (Luke 24:27)

Key Concept: God's Word

Materials: Bible, an adult or youth friend whom all the children know (optional)

(This sermon is written as if a friend was invited to be with the children. If you choose not to use this option, adapt the sermon for use with your children.) How many of you know my friend? *(Point to your friend and let the children answer.)* How did you know this person's name? *(Let the children respond.)* You know _____ because he/she is your friend too. You know his/her name because someone told you the first time you saw this person. We get to know people by being with them. We learn what their name is, what they look like, what they like to do, what they like to eat, and where they live. You know these things about your friends. Can you name a friend and tell us what he or she likes to do when you play together? *(Have the children raise their hands and call on two or three individually for examples.)* We know our friends because we listen, look, and spend time with them.

Jesus had friends. Some of his friends went out of town on that first Easter morning. While they were walking, Jesus came to them, but they didn't know who he was. Jesus walked with them and asked what they were talking about. One of them, Cleophas, told him everything that had happened. He was surprised that this stranger had not heard about Jesus' death on the cross. The travelers told the stranger that Jesus was a great man of God. Cleophas said that even the women had seen angels at the tomb that morning and learned that Jesus was alive. Peter and others went to look for Jesus, but his body was gone. They had hoped Jesus would save Israel, God's chosen people.

This stranger (whom we know is Jesus) began to tell the travelers what Old Testament prophets and older Scriptures said about the Messiah. Luke 24:27 says, *Then beginning with Moses and all the prophets, he [Jesus] interpreted to them the things about himself in all the scriptures.* The three of them kept on walking together.

Cleophas and his friend planned to stop for the night, but Jesus acted as though he would keep going. Cleophas invited the stranger to stay with them. This stranger knew so much about the Messiah. When they sat down to eat, Jesus broke the bread and gave thanks. Then he gave some bread to Cleophas and his friend. Suddenly, they recognized their friend Jesus, and he disappeared from their sight.

Just like these friends of Jesus, we can recognize Jesus when we hear Scripture stories *(and when we break and eat bread, if this is a part of your tradition for children).* We listen to the stories of Jesus so we can know about Jesus. The stories help us recognize when someone is being like Jesus because we learn what Jesus liked, what he talked about, and how he lived. *(You can include more here about the Lord's Table if that is a part of your tradition.)*

Day by Day

Date: Fourth Sunday of Easter

Scripture: Acts 2:42-47

Key Verse: They devoted themselves to the apostles' teaching and fellowship, to the breaking of bread and the prayers. . . . And day by day the Lord added to their number those who were being saved. (Acts 2:42, 47b)

Key Concept: Discipleship

Materials: Bible, box containing different and interesting hats

Preparation: Hide the box of hats behind the pulpit. Before the service, enlist two helpers and explain that during the children's sermon, you need them to look behind the pulpit and show a lot of enthusiasm for what they find. Tell them there is a box of hats (or whatever you choose to put in the box). Ask them to show excitement so the other children will want to see what they found. Tell the enlisted children to go to the box when you invite everyone up for the children's sermon.

I'm so glad you are here today. It's such a beautiful day. *(The children may notice that two of their friends have gone behind the pulpit and are talking. Some may actually go with them. If you see interest, or if the children begin to flock to the box, have your helpers bring the box so everyone can explore the contents. Let the activity continue as long as you are comfortable, allowing freedom to move without causing an inappropriate disruption.)*

Everyone became interested in what was in the box [*name*] and [*name*] found behind the pulpit. When others are having fun or exploring something new, we want to join them. I've been to places where strangers were having a party. Because they were having such a good time together, I wished I could have joined them.

(Open Bible.) In our Scripture from Acts 2:47, Luke wrote, *They devoted themselves to the apostles' teaching and fellowship, to the breaking of bread and the prayers ... And day by day the Lord added to their number those who were being saved.* The early church, the first church that followed Jesus' teachings, was only beginning. These people learned together, spent time together, prayed together, and ate together. They showed love and care toward each other. They didn't go out and invite people to join them, but

people saw what they were doing together. The Spirit of God was so much a part of these Christians that people came to know Jesus. When someone comes to know Jesus, we say they are saved. They are saved from their sinful ways and become followers or disciples of Jesus.

Has anyone told you to invite your friends to church? That is important. But today I want us to think about how we show others God's Spirit so they will want to come and be with us at church. How are people who love Jesus different from other people? *(Let the children respond.)* We are different in many ways from others who don't know Jesus. You named some of them. It's important for us to learn what Jesus wants us to do and say each day. We should take time to read our Bible. We should ask Jesus to help us be different so that others can see and want to know about Jesus. We want others to see how we love, share, learn, and live together as a special family. Maybe then they will be curious enough to come and see.

Lost and Found

Date: Fourth Sunday of Easter

Scripture: 1 Peter 2:19-25

Key Verse: For you were going astray like sheep, but now you have returned to the shepherd and guardian of your souls. (1 Peter 2:25)

Key Concepts: Sin and forgiveness

Materials: Bible

Have you ever been lost? *(Let the children answer. Allow one or two children to tell briefly about when they were lost.)* I remember thinking I was lost one time. It doesn't feel good. You feel alone and scared. You want to see your mom or your dad. It's a bad feeling. When you are found, it feels good. You feel safe again. You lose that scared feeling. You feel better. You are happy because you are with your family again.

Our passage talks about being lost. *(Open Bible.)* First Peter 2:25 says, *For you were going astray like sheep, but now you have returned to the shepherd and guardian of your souls.* Going astray means getting lost. This verse talks about sheep who are getting lost. Sheep need a lot of direction. They need a shepherd to help them get food and water. They need a shepherd for protection. They need a shepherd to get them from one place to another.

Do you know what a symbol is? A symbol is when you use one thing to describe something else because it makes it easier to understand. There were many shepherds and sheep during Bible times. People could understand verses like this one because they knew what it was like to care for sheep. Our Scripture speaks of Jesus as our shepherd. That makes us Jesus' sheep, since we are followers of Jesus. We need Shepherd Jesus to protect us and help us know how to follow him.

Our verse talks about going astray or getting lost. When we become lost from Jesus, it's because of sin. Sin is wrong thoughts, words, or actions that are not Jesus' way. When we sin, we are separated or lost from Jesus. But when we ask Jesus to forgive us, we're no longer lost. When we choose to think Jesus' way, we aren't lost. When we choose to act Jesus' way, we aren't lost. In fact, Jesus helps us come back to him because he loves us.

All Seasons

Date: Fifth Sunday of Easter

Scripture: Psalm 31:1-5, 15-16

Key Verse: My times are in your hand . . . . (Psalm 31:15a)

Key Concept: God's presence

Materials: Bible, calendar with pictures of all seasons, pictures of people experiencing various emotions

I brought a calendar today, and I'd like you to see the pretty pictures. *(Show the children one of the pictures depicting a season of the year.)* What season do you think this picture shows? *(Let the children respond. Continue showing the various pictures and asking the children which season is shown.)* These pictures show all the different seasons. Who made the seasons and the beautiful scenery we saw in the pictures? *(Let the children answer.)* God made all the seasons and all of creation. God made it for us to enjoy and take care of.

I brought more pictures. How does this person feel? *(Show the children the pictures that depict various emotions. Continue to ask the children until you have shown all the pictures.)* Who made us and gave us these different feelings? *(Let the children respond.)* God made us and gave us all kinds of feelings. Sometimes we are happy, and sometimes we are sad. We can be surprised and we can be afraid. God made us to feel different ways at different times.

(Open Bible.) Psalm 31:15 says, *My times are in your hand . . . .* The psalmist knew God was present—God was with the psalmist all the time and everywhere. I bet the person who wrote this psalm had times that were happy, sad, surprising, and even scary, but God was there all the time. The psalmist probably saw spring flowers, hot summers, cool fall nights, and winter snow. The psalmist knew God was there because God made all those things. The psalmist honored God by giving time to God. This person loved and trusted God every day, on good days and bad days.

God is with us each day. We can live and honor God just as the psalmist did. We can give our time to God each day. Even if we have a rotten day, we know God is with us. We can still honor God even when things are hard or sad. Remember that God made us and wants what is best for us. Praise God for every new day!

Praying in Jesus' Name

Date: Fifth Sunday of Easter

Scripture: John 14:1-14

Key Verse: If in my name you ask me for anything, I will do it. (John 14:14)

Key Concept: Praying in Jesus' name

Materials: Bible

When we pray together during worship, we usually end the prayer by saying "in Jesus' name." Why do you think we end our prayers that way? *(Let the children respond. Expect a variety of answers.)* These are good answers. *(Adapt as needed, depending on the answers you get.)*

One of the reasons we pray in Jesus' name is because of something Jesus said in the Gospel of John. *(Open Bible.)* In John 14:14, Jesus said to his disciples, *If in my name you ask me for anything, I will do it.* In Scripture, Jesus told us to pray in his name. Jesus even told his disciples that through prayer they would be able to do greater things than he did. Jesus did great things like healing the sick and feeding people who were hungry.

When Jesus taught his disciples, he also taught them how to pray. We know this prayer as the Lord's Prayer.

Jesus said he would do anything we ask in his name. I think he meant for us to pray for what he wants the world to be like. We can pray for peace, for the hungry to have food, for the homeless to have a place to stay, and for every person to act out of love for each other. We say something like this in the Lord's Prayer: "Your kingdom come." Let this world be like Jesus wants it to be.

We need to remember that Jesus didn't teach us to be selfish and pray for what we want, but for what Jesus wants. It is easy to pray to Jesus for a new toy or something we want. It's not what we want that counts, but what Jesus wants for all of us. *(Be aware that some children already question how God answers prayer. They may wonder why God hasn't answered their prayers for peace in the world, etc. Be prepared for such questions.)*

Come and Hear

Date: Sixth Sunday of Easter

Scripture: Psalm 66:8-20

Key Verse: Come and hear, all you who fear God, and I will tell what he has done for me. (Psalm 66:16)

Key Concept: Telling others about God

Materials: Bible, symbols from your baptism and other moments when God moved in your life

Preparation: The first portion of the sermon is my personal story. Please use my example to prepare your own story and symbols of what God has done for you.

I want to tell you about special things God has done for me. These items help me remember those special times. First, I want to show you this certificate. My parents got this certificate when they dedicated me at church. They promised to bring me to church and teach me God's ways all my life. God gave me special parents who did that for me. They told me stories from the Bible and showed me God's way and God's love.

Here is another certificate. I got this certificate when I was baptized. I remember that special day. I remember saying I wanted to follow Jesus' way instead of my way. I was glad to be Jesus' follower and belong to God's church in a new way. God helped me do that.

Here is a picture. It shows my husband and me on the day we got married. God gave me a special friend who became my husband. I love him very much and thank God that God gave me such a special partner with whom to share my life.

I have three more pictures to show you. They are pictures of Nathanael, Andrew, and Matthew. They're the children God gave to Mr. Philip and me. It was so exciting to become parents the first, second, and third times. Each son is a wonderful gift God gave to me. God has done so many things for me and given me so much to be thankful for.

(Open Bible.) Psalm 66:16 says, *Come and hear, all you who fear God, and I will tell what he has done for me.* Just like the psalmist, we can tell others what God has done for us. He has given you moms and dads, brothers and sisters. He has given you a home and food, and this special

church family that helps you know even more about what God has done. I told you some of the special things God has done for me. You can tell what God has done for you. Raise your hand if you'd like to tell something that God has done for you. *(Let the children respond, guiding them if they need help. Then use what the children say to lead a prayer that includes some of the special things God has done for them.)*

How Do We Tell?

Date: Sixth Sunday of Easter

Scripture: 1 Peter 3:13-22

Key Verses: Always be ready to make your defense to anyone who demands from you an accounting for the hope that is in you; yet do it with gentleness and reverence. (1 Peter 3:15b-16a)

Key Concept: Telling the good news

Materials: Bible

I want to tell you a story. It's about a boy named Tim and his older brother Charlie. One day Tim decided he could get Charlie in trouble. Charlie sat in the living room reading a book. Their mom and dad sat in the kitchen next to the living room. Tim came into the room, walked over to Charlie, and hit him on the head. Then Tim ran into the other room holding his head. He told his parents Charlie had hit him on the head. Charlie wasn't sure how to tell his parents that Tim had hit him instead. He tried to figure out what to say, but he didn't think they would believe him. He tried to tell his parents what happened. He defended himself, which means he tried to help his parents understand what really happened.

Has your sister, brother, or a friend ever told on you? You try to defend yourself by telling your side of the story. Sometimes you did what the other person said you did. Sometimes you didn't. Either way, you like to have a chance to tell what happened. When you defend yourself, you explain what you think happened.

(Open Bible.) First Peter 3:15b-16a says, *Always be ready to make your defense to anyone who demands from you an accounting for the hope that is in you; yet do it with gentleness and reverence.* We need to be ready at any time to tell others why we love and follow Jesus. This is what it means to account for our hope. When others see that you follow Jesus, they may want to know more about him. If we tell others about Jesus, we must talk with gentleness and reverence. This means we treat the other person the way we want to be treated—kindly and with respect.

If anyone asks you why you follow Jesus, kindly tell him or her why you love and follow Jesus. It might help the person know and love Jesus too.

Make Us One

Date: Seventh Sunday of Easter

Scripture: John 17:1-11

Key Verse: Holy Father, protect them in your name that you have given me, so that they may be one, as we are one. (John 17:11b)

Key Concept: Unity

Materials: Bible, Lego® building blocks (enough to build one vehicle), self-sealing bags

Preparation: Place Lego blocks in four separate bags, being sure not to give any group enough blocks to build the vehicle. You may want to provide a building kit with specific instructions on how to construct the vehicle. The choir may participate as described below.

I'm going to give each group some Lego blocks, and I want you to build the car you see on this instruction sheet. *(Form three or four groups and give each group a bag of Lego blocks and instructions. Let them build until they tell you they do not have all the pieces. Assure them you brought enough pieces. If the groups do not begin working together, lead them to ask other groups if they have certain pieces. Encourage them to work together until the vehicle is finished.)*

You had to work together as a team to finish the car. One group had the wheels; another had the body of the car *(etc.)*. None of the groups had enough blocks to make the car on their own.

(Open Bible.) Jesus prayed for his disciples to work together. In John 17:11b he says, *Holy Father, protect them in your name that you have given me, so that they may be one, as we are one.* Jesus knew it would be hard to tell the good news. Not everyone wanted to hear about Jesus' way. The disciples were Jesus' friends. He knew that if they worked together, each of them could give something to the whole group that would help spread Jesus' way.

When we work together, we call it unity. Another word for unity is harmony. It's more than getting along with each other. Each person does his or her part. When we listen to our choir sing, they don't always sing the same note at the same time. The music is beautiful when the different parts come together to make harmony. *(Consider demonstrating harmony with one chord.*

Let each section in the choir sing their note separately, and then let them sing it all together.)

Jesus wants us to work together as a church. When we come together to build a Habitat house, we work together in harmony. Each person has a special talent to help create the house. *(You may want to insert an example here that fits your church's ministry.)* When we make choices as a church about how to spend our money, we put it together to do things that we couldn't do alone. There are so many ways we can work together in unity. You do your part when you give an offering and do church activities. You are a part of this family called *(church name)*. This church family works together to be one as Jesus said. We also work with other churches to be one in the ministry of Jesus.

God Cares for You

Date: Seventh Sunday of Easter

Scripture: 1 Peter 4:12-14; 5:6-11

Key Verse: Cast all your anxiety on him, because he cares for you. (1 Peter 5:7)

Key Concept: God's care and protection

Materials: Bible, current newspaper

Preparation: Browse through the newspaper for articles that depict worries children have (i.e., war, lost pets, car accidents, stormy weather, etc.).

(Open Bible.) Our verse for today is from 1 Peter 5:7. It says, *Cast all your anxiety on him, because he cares for you.* Anxiety means worry or fear. What do you worry about? What scares you? *(Let the children share their worries and fears. Repeat their answers so they know you heard them and so others in the congregation can learn some of the children's fears and worries.)* So many things can worry us and scare us. Sometimes it's hard to tell someone your worries and fears.

I brought a newspaper. Let's see if there are worries in the paper. *(Hold up the paper and show them different problems that have happened in the nation and the world. Explain them on a child's level.)*

We've talked about our personal worries. We've looked at the newspaper and found other problems that worry us or make us afraid. I want you to know God cares for you. Because of that, we can pray to God about our worries and fears. God cares for us and wants what's best for us. Let's go to God in prayer and tell God our worries and fears. Let's ask God to help us to feel God's love and care as we pray. *(Lead the children in a time of prayer. Pray specifically for their fears and worries. Pray also for the worries that were found in the paper.)*

Say It!

Date: *Pentecost*

Scripture: *1 Corinthians 12:3b-13*

Key Verse: *. . . and no one can say "Jesus is Lord" except by the Holy Spirit.*
   (1 Corinthians 12:3b)

Key Concept: *Holy Spirit/Pentecost*

Materials: *Bible, blindfold*

I need two volunteers. *(Choose two children who won't mind touching each other.)* I'm going to blindfold *Ellie*, and *Savannah* will lead her up the aisle and back down the other side. *(Let the children begin their journey around the sanctuary. Once they return, have them sit with the others.)*

When Savannah helped Ellie around the sanctuary, we could have called her a guide. Savannah guided Ellie around the sanctuary. She helped Ellie know when to go forward and when to turn. What would happen if Ellie decided not to listen to Savannah? *(Let the children respond.)* She would have run into things and might have gotten hurt. We need a guide to help us each day. God gave us a guide—the Holy Spirit.

Today is Pentecost. We celebrate Pentecost because that's when the early Christians were given the Holy Spirit. Jesus told his disciples that he would send the Holy Spirit to guide and teach all Christians. *(Open Bible.)* Paul wrote the Christians in the early church. He wrote, *. . . and no one can say "Jesus is Lord" except by the Holy Spirit.* Paul taught that the Holy Spirit helps us say "Jesus is Lord." The Holy Spirit guides us or gives us direction to know God's way. When Ellie was blindfolded, she needed directions to get from one place to another. We need the Holy Spirit to help us choose the right way—God's way in the things we do and say.

Common Lectionary
Year B

A Rainbow of Promise

Date: First Sunday in Lent

Scripture: Genesis 9:8-17

Key Verse: I have set my bow in the clouds, and it shall be a sign of the covenant between me and the earth. (Genesis 9:13)

Key Concepts: God's covenant

Materials: Bible, prism with light source (optional) or picture of a rainbow, paper, crayons or markers

Preparation: If you use a prism, show the children how it makes the colors of the rainbow by reflecting the image of colors on a piece of paper. Consider writing the mnemonic ROY G BIV on a white piece of paper. Write each letter in the color it represents (see below).

Have any of you ever seen a rainbow in the sky? *(Let the children share.)* Rainbows are beautiful. When I was your age, I loved to draw big beautiful rainbows. Then when I got older and studied science in school, I learned a way to remember the order of the colors of the rainbow: ROY G BIV. *(Hold up the poster you made.)* It sounds like a funny name, but it helped me remember the colors. *(Let the children respond after each of the following questions.)* R is for red. What is red in God's creation? O is for orange. What is orange in God's creation? Y is for yellow. What is yellow in God's creation? G is for green. What is green in God's creation? B is for blue. What is blue in God's creation? I is for indigo. This color is bluish-purple. Can you think of anything indigo in God's creation? V is for violet or purple. What is violet in God's creation?

God has created many wonderful things in the colors of the rainbow. Today, our lesson comes from the story of Noah. Who can tell me what happened to Noah? *(Choose a volunteer to tell the story. Fill in gaps if necessary.)* At the end of the story, God makes a promise to Noah and all of creation. *(Open Bible.)* In Genesis 9:13, God says, *I have set my bow in the clouds, and it shall be a sign of the covenant between me and the earth*. God said the rainbow would be a reminder to God of God's promise or covenant. God promised that water would never again cover the whole earth at once.

The rainbow is a loving act of God for us, too. Every time you see a rainbow, you can remember God's love for you and God's promise to take care of you. Because of God's promise of love and grace, we can be thankful.

(End with a simple prayer, thanking God for promises and for sending Jesus.)

Waiting for God to Teach

Date: First Sunday in Lent

Scripture: Psalm 25:1-10

Key Verse: Lead me in your truth, and teach me, for you are the God of my salvation; for you I wait all day long. (Psalm 25:5)

Key Concepts: Following God's ways

Materials: Bible

Have you ever had to wait all day for something to happen? *(Let the children respond.)* I remember taking long trips to my grandparents' house. We rode in a car for an entire day. I was always excited to go and see them. It seemed like the clock stopped and the miles went by slowly. I didn't visit my grandparents often, but I remember how I looked forward to seeing them while we drove. Some of you may have had to wait all day for a birthday party or to open presents at Christmas. We want fun things to happen right now, don't we? Do you ever get excited about fun things? *(Let the children respond.)*

(Open Bible.) In our Scripture lesson today, the person who wrote Psalm 25 felt the same way. Instead of a party or presents or a special activity, this writer, whom we believe was David, wanted to learn God's ways. David knew he had much to learn about God. He also knew he didn't always do what God wanted him to do. God could forgive his sin.

David prayed this prayer because he knew God loved him and cared for him. In verse 5, he says, *Lead me in your truth, and teach me, for you are the God of my salvation; for you I wait all day long.* David asked God to help him. He was excited about God! He wanted God to show him the truth and help him learn to live it. He wanted it so much that he would wait all day long for God. God keeps promises; God is faithful.

This is the first Sunday of Lent. During Lent, we ask God to teach us truths. It's a time to get ready for Easter. We can think about how we live each day and if we are following God's ways. The good news is that God loves us and forgives us. Like David, we should pray and try to learn new lessons from God every day. You can read your Bible and pray with your family.

Let's be like David and want to know God's ways so much that we get excited! God will be faithful and teach us if we seek to know.

Worship God

Date: Second Sunday in Lent

Scripture: Psalm 22:23-31

Key Verse: All the ends of the earth shall remember and turn to the Lord; and all the families of the nations shall worship before him. (Psalm 22:27)

Key Concepts: Worshiping God

Materials: Bible, pictures of people from around the world, globe

Preparation: Find pictures of people of varying status all around the world and be able to show the children the various locations on the globe.

I brought pictures for you to see. *(Consider choosing a child to help you show the various items.)* This is a picture from *(name location)*. On the globe, that place is located here. *(Show the children the pictures and the various places you chose. Show the children where they live in relation to the other locations.)* God made many different kinds of people who live all over the world. Each of these people and countries are special to God.

(Open Bible.) In Psalm 22, David writes that God is the God of all people. God wants everyone to know of God's love. In verse 27, David writes, *All the ends of the earth shall remember and turn to the LORD; and all the families of the nations shall worship before him.* This is a perfect picture of the way God made us to be. What would it be like if every person in the world worshiped and loved God?

People in every country have leaders. In America, we have a president and helpers who make big decisions. We pray for them to make right choices. But God is the leader or ruler of the whole earth. God made everything, and everything is God's. Not everybody knows about God. We don't have to go to other countries to find people who don't know God. They live here in our town/city. How can we help others know the joy of worshiping God? *(Let the children answer.)* The best way to start is to worship God every day in our own families. We can tell others about God through the way we live. We can also become friends with them and invite them to worship with us.

Everyone in every place is special to God. Remember God each day and worship God together as a family. This is the best way to thank God and show our love for God.

You Can Count on It

Date: Second Sunday in Lent

Scripture: Romans 4:13-25

Key Verses: . . . he grew strong in his faith as he gave glory to God, being fully convinced that God was able to do what he had promised. (Romans 4:20b-21)

Key Concept: God's faithfulness

Materials: Bible

When I was four years old, I remember my parents telling me they were going to play "bridge." I always wished I could go with them to play, even though I didn't understand that it was a card game. When they talked about playing bridge, I thought they went somewhere to crawl across a bridge! Sometimes words and phrases mean different things at different times. Have you ever heard anyone say, "You can count on it"? This phrase doesn't mean exactly what you might think it means. You might think it means counting something: 1, 2, 3, 4, 5. Instead, it means that what someone said would happen will actually happen. It's like a promise.

In Genesis and Romans in the Bible, we learn about Abraham. When Abraham was an old man, God told him that he and his elderly wife Sarah would have a child. More importantly, Abraham would have as many descendants as the stars in the sky. Descendants are children, grandchildren, great-grandchildren, great-great-grandchildren, and so on. Even though it seemed impossible, God said to Abraham, "You can count on it; this will happen." Abraham believed because he had strong faith in God. Paul wrote that Abraham knew God would keep this promise. *(Open Bible.)* In Romans 4:20b-21, Paul writes, . . . *but he grew strong in his faith as he gave glory to God, being fully convinced that God was able to do what he had promised.*

It was a miracle that Abraham and Sarah had a baby. God was faithful. God kept the promise even when it seemed impossible. God is the same today. God is faithful to us and loves us so much. You can count on it!

Word Power

Date: *Third Sunday in Lent*

Scripture: *Psalm 19*

Key Verse: *Let the words of my mouth and the meditation of my heart be acceptable to you, O Lord, my rock and my redeemer. (Psalm 19:14)*

Key Concept: *Pleasing God*

Materials: *Bible, index cards, marker*

Preparation: *Using different colors of markers, print the following words on index cards, one word per card: love, hate, ugly, beautiful, mean, good.*

I hope everyone is having a rotten day! I don't want to see anybody smiling or laughing either. (*Pretend you are in a terrible mood. If the children laugh, act as if they are ruining your already bad day. After a few moments, change your tone and continue.*) You know what I said isn't true. I don't want anybody to have a rotten day, and I love to see smiles and hear laughter. But our words can have power over people. It doesn't make us feel good to hear someone say hurtful words.

I brought word cards this morning. Can someone help me? (*Choose several volunteers and give each child a card. Have them take turns reading the word on their card. Assist as necessary. Ask all the children to talk about how each word makes them feel.*) _____ has the word "hate." How do you feel when you hear that word? (*Let the children answer. Read each card and do the same.*)

David wrote a hymn about God. He said God is our creator and the one who gave the law found in the Bible. (*Open Bible.*) In Psalm 19:14, David writes, *Let the words of my mouth and the meditation of my heart be acceptable to you, O LORD, my rock and my redeemer.* This was David's prayer that everything he said and thought about would please God. When we say hurtful things, we aren't pleasing God. Our words and our thoughts tell others about who we are. People are called bullies if they always want their way and hurt others to get it.

As we continue to get ready for Easter, let's remember to say kind and thoughtful words to those around us. Let's help others know we are followers of God and please God with all we say and do.

Let's pray. I'll use the verse as our prayer. (*Read verse 14 again.*)

Jesus' Zeal

Date: Third Sunday in Lent

Scripture: John 2:13-22

Key Verses: He told those who were selling the doves, "Take these things out of here! Stop making my Father's house a marketplace!" His disciples remembered that it was written, "Zeal for your house will consume me." (John 2:16-17)

Key Concept: Jesus' identity

Materials: Bible, adult to perform monologue as a seller in the market

Preparation: Invite an adult to dress in biblical attire and perform the monologue printed below. Give that person a copy of the monologue early in the week.

Today we have a visitor from long ago. He was in Jerusalem when Jesus came to town for Passover. He sold animals to people who wanted to sacrifice at the temple. *(If necessary, explain that a sacrifice was a gift to God so that God would forgive a person's sins. When Jesus died for us, he became the sacrifice for all of us forever.)* Here he comes. Let's listen to what he says about Jesus.

Monologue

Hello, young friends. My name is Daniel. I live in Jerusalem. I sell animals to people who are going to sacrifice in the temple.

One day, we set up our tables in the temple as usual. People came and went, buying some of our items. Jesus also came that day. I saw him from a distance, and I could tell he was upset. I thought someone had cheated him. Then all of the sudden, he knocked over a table. Everyone was surprised.

"Take these things out of here!" Jesus shouted. "Stop making my Father's house a marketplace!"

Some of the people began asking him questions. I packed up my things and moved out of the temple. Jesus had zeal. Zeal means caring deeply about something, being excited about it, and working hard to protect it. Jesus had zeal about the temple. It really was his Father's house.

Many of us forgot why the temple was important. We only wanted to make money. We forgot about God. Jesus reminded us that day. Some of us changed, but many people stayed the same. They couldn't understand that Jesus was God's Son, the one we wanted to come and save us.

(Open Bible.) I talked with Jesus' disciples and they reminded me of Psalm 69:9, which says, *It is zeal for your house that has consumed me.* Jesus had zeal. Maybe we all need a little more zeal about God's church. *(Exit)*

Daniel's story comes from the Gospel of John. Jesus' words and actions told about who he was. He was in his Father's house, and he was God's Son. His zeal or passion showed what was important. He wanted people to know who he was and that God's house was a holy place of worship. As we continue to prepare during Lent, we need to learn more about who Jesus is. Have zeal—take time each day to read stories of Jesus so you will know more about who Jesus is.

A Gathered Thankful People

Date: Fourth Sunday in Lent

Scripture: Psalm 107:1-3, 17-22

*Key Verses: O give thanks to the Lord, for he is good; for his steadfast love
endures forever. Let the redeemed of the Lord say so, those he
redeemed from trouble and gathered in from the lands, from the east
and from the west, from the north and from the south. (Psalm 107:1-3)*

Key Concepts: Thankfulness, God's love

Materials: Bible, compass

*Preparation: Prior to Sunday, test the compass in the sanctuary. See how
much the compass moves as you walk in various directions. Print the
words from verse 1 in the bulletin for congregation participation. If
your hymnal includes songs that use this verse, sing it to one of the
tunes. Otherwise, make up a simple tune. Ask your music minister for
assistance.*

Let's begin by reading part of Psalm 107. I brought my Bible. Would
someone like to read three verses for me? *(Choose a child who can read Ps
107:1-3, 17-22. Consider asking an older child ahead of time to be prepared to
read. Or read it to the children yourself.)*

This is a song of thankfulness God's people sang long ago. They knew
God loved them. We can sing this song of thankfulness, too. We know God
loves us all the time. Yesterday, today, tomorrow, next month, next year, and
forever—God loves us. This is a reason to be thankful.

Let's sing the first verse with the congregation. *(Consider having your
music minister sing the verse and lead the congregation through it one time.)*

We are going sing this verse in a special way. I brought a compass
today. *(Show the children the compass and the different directions.)* We are
going to move around the sanctuary and sing with those sitting in the east,
west, north, and south. I'll lead you around the sanctuary, and we'll ask
each group to sing with us. Then we'll all sing the song together. *(Lead the
children around the church—east, west, north, and south—and then gather
back at the front.)*

God's love is so great that we all come to this room each Sunday and
worship together. We are thankful for everything God has done for us.

Our Life, A Big Thank You

Date: Fourth Sunday in Lent

Scripture: Ephesians 2:1-10

Key Verses: For by grace you have been saved through faith, and this is not your own doing; it is the gift of God—not the result of works, so that no one may boast. For we are what he has made us, created in Christ Jesus for good works, which God prepared beforehand to be our way of life. (Ephesians 2:8-10)

Key Concepts: Salvation, thankfulness

Materials: Bible, one piece of posterboard folded vertically to resemble a large greeting card, markers

When someone does something nice for you, what do you say? *(Let the children answer.)* We say *thank you.* Sometimes we even send a thank-you note to someone. This is a way to show how much we like and appreciate what they gave us. Have any of you ever written a thank-you note? *(Let the children respond.)* I brought a big blank thank-you note. Who do you think we need to thank? *(Let the children answer.)*

Let's write a thank-you note to God. In our Bible reading from Ephesians 2, Paul says, *For by grace you have been saved through faith, and this is not your own doing; it is the gift of God—not the result of works, so that no one may boast. For we are what he has made us, created in Christ for good works, which God prepared beforehand to be our way of life.*

Because we have faith in Jesus and believe in him, God gave us salvation. This means God forgave our sins and promises that we will be with God forever. This is the best gift anyone could give. When God saves us, we want to do good things for God. Jesus helps us do good things. The way we live—what we do and say—is our way of thanking God for the promises and gifts God gives us. Everything we have comes from God.

On this thank-you note, I will write ways that we can show God our thankfulness. We'll keep this note up front today as a reminder of how we can live our lives Jesus' way. Can you tell me some ways we can show our thankfulness to God with the way we live? *(Let the children respond as you write their answers in different colors. Assist them with suggestions as needed. If suitable for your service, you can let children write or draw their own answers on the posterboard.)*

As we continue to get ready for Easter, it's good to think about how we can thank God through the way we act and the things we say to our family and friends. Let's try to remember how thankful we are for Jesus and for the chance to live with him forever.

Glued to It

Date: Fifth Sunday in Lent

Scripture: Psalm 119:9-16

Key Verse: I will meditate on your precepts, and fix my eyes on your ways. (Psalm 119:15)

Key Concepts: God's Word, God's way

Materials: Bible, glue/something to glue together

Why do we use glue? *(Let the children respond.)* I brought a _____. I need to glue the pieces together. Can one of you help me? *(Choose a child to help.)* We use glue to make things stick to each other. These pieces hold together now, don't they?

Our verse for today is about gluing ourselves to God's Word and God's way. Psalm 119:15 says, *I will meditate on your precepts, and fix my eyes on your ways.* The word *glue* is not in this verse, but let's think about what the verse means. *Precepts* means God's word or law. If we meditate on God's word, we think deeply about it. We might say we glue ourselves to it. This doesn't mean we use real glue like we did to make these pieces stick. It means we want to stick close to God's Word so we can know more about God and God's way for us. We should read and keep our minds on God's Word.

Some of your parents might say, "You're glued to the TV." They don't mean you are stuck to the TV with real glue. They mean you are watching something and are interested in it. You can't take your eyes off it.

If we speak of fixing our eyes on God's ways, we might say we are glued to God's ways. We are always trying to do what God wants us to do.

Easter is only two weeks away. As we continue to get ready for Easter, let's try to "glue" ourselves to God's Word. This means we must study it and read it with our families. Let's keep our eyes glued to Jesus' way so we can show others we belong to him.

What's a Covenant?

Date: Fifth Sunday in Lent

Scripture: Jeremiah 31:31-34

Key Verses: But this is the covenant that I will make with the house of Israel after those days, says the Lord: I will put my law within them, and I will write it on their hearts; and I will be their God, and they shall be my people. No longer shall they teach one another, or say to each other, "Know the Lord," for they shall all know me, from the least of them to the greatest, says the Lord; for I will forgive their iniquity, and remember their sin no more. (Jeremiah 31:33-34)

Key Concepts: Covenant, forgiveness

Materials: Bible, marriage certificate, baptismal certificate, legal will, church covenant (use the items you have readily available)

Today I brought a copy of my marriage certificate. This piece of paper says that I'm married to my husband/wife, _____. It gives the date and the names of ministers who helped us take our vows. When we took our vows, we made promises to each other. Another word for promise is covenant.

This is another example of a covenant. This piece of paper shows our church covenant. When people want to join our church, these are the promises we make to each other. *(Read a small excerpt from the covenant. Show other certificates if you have them.)* When we make promises, we want to try to keep them.

In our lesson from Jeremiah, we learn about the covenant God made with God's chosen people, the people of Israel. Jeremiah 31:33-34 says, *But this is the covenant that I will make with the house of Israel after those days, says the LORD: I will put my law within them, and I will write it on their hearts; and I will be their God, and they shall be my people. No longer shall they teach one another, or say to each other, "Know the LORD," for they shall all know me, from the least of them to the greatest, says the LORD; for I will forgive their iniquity, and remember their sin no more.*

Long before Jeremiah was born, God made a covenant—a promise with God's people through Moses. It was the Ten Commandments. These laws helped God's people be faithful. They had to follow the commandments. The commandments grew into more and more laws. Soon, the people were busy trying to follow every single law. Some of them gave up because there were too many laws to follow. They forgot God. They didn't follow God's way or listen to God's messengers.

Jeremiah was one of God's messengers. He talked about God's new covenant. The people would desire this covenant. God would forgive the people's sins and never remember them again. We know God always keeps promises. God would do this for God's people.

We read this passage today because we see the new promise—the new covenant in Jesus. Because of Jesus, our sins are forgiven. Jesus shows us the way to live the new promise. If we try to be like Jesus, then everyone we meet will know the Lord. They will see Jesus in us through the things we say and do.

Shouting Hosanna!

Date: Sixth Sunday in Lent (Palm Sunday)

Scripture: Mark 11:1-11

Key Verses: Then those who went ahead and those who followed were shouting, "Hosanna! Blessed is the one who comes in the name of the Lord! Blessed is the coming kingdom of our ancestor David! Hosanna in the highest heaven!" (Mark 11:9-10)

Key Concepts: Palm Sunday, Jesus

Materials: Bible, broomstick horse, palm branches, coats

Preparation: The children will dramatize today's Scripture. Consider asking one child ahead of time to portray Jesus. Get real palm branches from a florist, and provide coats that can get a bit dirty. Read through the sermon carefully and consider asking several adults to be available to assist you.

Today, we're going to pretend we are outside of Jerusalem. _____ has agreed to be Jesus. I want you (*choose two children*) to be Jesus' disciples. You will go and get the colt for Jesus to ride. The rest of you will be the people following and going ahead of Jesus. You will say, "Hosanna! Here comes the Lord! Hosanna!" Let's practice.

(Repeat the phrase and let the children practice. Give them coats and palm branches to spread along an aisle floor. Explain that they will place these on the aisle as Jesus comes down. Ask Jesus and his disciples to go to the back of the church, and guide the other children to space themselves along the aisle. Place the broomstick horse at the front of the church. Consider asking other adults to help you place the children.)

(Speak this portion slowly, waiting for the children to act it out.) You will act out this story as I tell it. One day Jesus was on his way to Jerusalem. He sent his two special disciples ahead of him to get a colt in the village. The disciples got the colt and brought it back to Jesus. When they brought it back, they threw some of their coats on the colt. Other people began to place coats and palm branches on the path as Jesus made his way toward Jerusalem. Some of the people followed and some went ahead. They all shouted: *(Cue the children.)* "Hosanna! Here comes the Lord! Hosanna!"

Jesus entered Jerusalem and went to the temple. Because it was late, he then went to Bethany with his disciples.

I want you all to come back here for a moment. Thank you for acting out our story. It comes from Mark 11:1-11 in the New Testament. *(Open Bible and show the children.)* This story is the beginning of the last week in Jesus' life that leads us to Easter Sunday.

Today is called Palm Sunday. Why do you think we call it that? *(Let the children answer.)* The people were ready to make Jesus their king, and they had a big parade for him. Today we remember this special parade. We shout hosanna for Jesus. I hope each of you can shout hosanna, because Jesus is our friend and loves us very much.

Good News Reminders

Date: Easter Sunday

Scripture: 1 Corinthians 15:1-11

Key Verse: Now I would remind you, brothers and sisters, of the good news that I proclaimed to you, which you in turn received, in which also you stand . . . . (1 Corinthians 15:1)

Key Concept: Easter

Materials: Bible, take-home reminders for children: three plastic eggs per child with German saying attached (see below), globe

We all enjoy hunting for Easter eggs. Have you ever wondered why we have Easter eggs? It was a custom in many European countries to decorate Easter eggs with Christian symbols. People would paint beautiful pictures of the cross, butterflies that stood for new life, and other items that made them think of what Jesus did for us.

In the Ukraine *(point to the location on the globe)*, people make beautiful Easter eggs and give them as gifts. In Poland, they call the Easter eggs *pisanki*. During the week before Easter, Polish Christians decorate their *pisanki* and cook traditional foods. This week is more important than preparing for Christmas.

Easter eggs came to the United States when the Dutch came to settle here. As early as 1789, Easter eggs were decorated with scratch carving by the Pennsylvania Dutch. A sharp knife or pointed tool scratched the dye surface and created a beautiful design on the eggs.

Easter eggs can remind us of this great day we call Easter. We celebrate that Jesus is alive. *(Open Bible.)* In 1 Corinthians 15:1, Paul reminded people about the good news of Easter: *Now I would remind you, brothers and sisters, of the good news that I proclaimed to you, which you in turn received, in which also you stand . . . .*

Easter is the most important day for Christians. It is a day of great joy. I want to follow a German custom and give each of you three Easter eggs with the following verse attached: *All good things are three, Therefore I present you three Easter Eggs: Faith and Hope together with Charity, Never lose from the Heart, Faith to the Church; Hope in God, And Love Him to thy death* (from Priscilla Lord and Daniel Foley, *Easter the World Over* [Philadelphia: Chilton Book Co., 1971]). Happy Easter!

They Saw for Us

Date: Second Sunday of Easter

Scripture: John 20:19-31

Key Verses: Jesus said to him, "Have you believed because you have seen me? Blessed are those who have not seen and yet have come to believe." Now Jesus did many other signs in the presence of the disciples, which are not written in this book. But these are written so that you may come to believe that Jesus is the Messiah and that through believing you may have life in his name. (John 20:29-31)

Key Concepts: Faith, God's Word

Materials: Bible, electric fan

Today I brought a fan. We will turn it on and make wind blow indoors. *(Turn on the fan and let it blow on the children.)* Can you see air move? *(Let the children respond. You may get all sorts of answers.)* We can't see the air move. We know the blades of the fan pull in air and push it out so we can feel a breeze, but we can't see the air move. On a windy day, we can't see the air move, but we can feel it and see the trees move because of the wind. We believe the wind blows, but we can't see it. Can you think of other things that we can't see, but we know they are real? *(Let the children respond.)* When we believe in and trust something or someone to be real, we say we have faith.

Our lesson for today talks about believing without seeing. *(Open Bible.)* In John 20:29-31, Jesus speaks to Thomas: *Jesus said to him, "Have you believed because you have seen me? Blessed are those who have not seen and yet have come to believe." Now Jesus did many other signs in the presence of the disciples, which are not written in this book. But these are written so that you may come to believe that Jesus is the Messiah, the Son of God, and that through believing you may have life in his name.* Jesus said that those who believe in him even though they cannot see him are blessed. When we have faith in Jesus—when we believe and trust him—we are blessed.

We haven't seen Jesus as a person the way the disciples did. The writer of John lets us "see" Jesus through his writing. He wanted us to know that Jesus is the Messiah and the Son of God. The disciples saw Jesus, told others about him, and wrote down what they saw so we can see Jesus, too.

In the Bible, we can read the stories of Jesus and learn what Jesus did and how he lived. The people who wrote the stories in the Bible saw for us. We can read and see pictures in our minds of what it might have been like to be with Jesus. Because we believe and trust Jesus, we are blessed.

Together

Date: *Second Sunday of Easter*

Scripture: *Psalm 133*

Key Verse: *How very good and pleasant it is when kindred live together in unity! (Psalm 133:1)*

Key Concept: *Unity*

Materials: *Bible, cookies (enough to give each child 3 or 4 cookies)*

I brought cookies with me today. I want each of you to have one. *(Give each child one cookie.)* I'm feeling generous today. Here, have another one. *(Give each child another cookie.)* I don't think you have enough yet. I need to give you two more. I think I'll give them all away. *(Give the children two or more cookies depending on how many you have left. Make sure each child gets the same number.)*

There is a reason that I gave you all those cookies. When we give more than we have to, we are being generous. When someone gives and gives and gives, we say they are generous. Another word we might use is *extravagant.* This is how the psalmist in today's psalm described being together as a family. *(Open Bible.)* Psalm 133:1 says, *How very good and pleasant it is when kindred live together in unity!* The togetherness of a family was described as extravagant when they lived in unity. Another word for unity is working together or agreeing. The psalmist described unity as "precious oil" being poured over a person. In biblical times, there was not much oil. Oil cost a lot of money. Pouring oil over a person meant you were so full of joy that you did something extravagant. I was extravagant when I gave you a lot of cookies.

We are God's family. God wants us to live, work, and worship together in unity or agreement. God created us to share life together. What joy and blessings we have when we live together in unity. It becomes extravagant. It's more than we need.

Eyewitness

Date: Third Sunday of Easter

Scripture: Luke 24:36-48

Key Verse: You are witnesses of these things. (Luke 24:48)

Key Concept: Learning about Jesus

Materials: Bible

Preparation: Invite someone to perform an unusual talent, such as juggling, magic tricks, etc. Let it be something the children can see visually.

I invited _____ to show us something special today. *(Ask the person to share his or her talent at this time.)* Was it exciting to see _____ do _____? I could tell that you enjoyed it. What did you see? *(Let the children respond. Ask for details.)*

When we see something and can tell what we saw, we are witnesses. You witnessed this trick, and maybe you can tell your friends about it at school, even though they weren't here to see it. You know what happened and you can describe what you saw. *(Open Bible.)* In Luke 24:48, Jesus tells the disciples this, *You are witnesses of these things.* The disciples witnessed things Jesus did while he was here on earth. They got to meet Jesus in person and see what happened as he went from place to place healing, feeding, and teaching the people around him. They were eyewitnesses. They saw everything and could tell what happened.

How do we see Jesus? *(Let the children answer. Reflect back their answers.)* The disciples told other people about Jesus, and the church grew. The church members told other people, and those people told other people, and those people told other people all through history until now. The story of Jesus was written for us. We find it in our Bible in the New Testament books of Matthew, Mark, Luke, and John. We can see Jesus when others do kind things for us because they are Christians. We can see Jesus when we come to church and study, worship, and pray. We can learn about Jesus, and we can be witnesses too. We can share the love of Jesus with others every day.

God's Children

Date: Third Sunday of Easter

Scripture: 1 John 3:1-7

Key Verse: See what love the Father has given us, that we should be called children of God; and that is what we are. (1 John 3:1a)

Key Concept: God's love

Materials: Bible

Preparation: Enlist a couple with a baby to help with the children's sermon. Ask them to prepare to share with the children things they do for their child and why.

I have invited Mr. & Mrs. _____ and their baby, _____, to come and help us this morning. Please listen carefully to what they tell you. I asked them to tell you about the things they do for their baby. *(Invite the parents to share things they do for their baby, such as feeding, changing, carrying, providing toys, etc. Have them emphasize their love for the child.)*

Mr. & Mrs. _____ have to do a lot of things for _____. They do those things because they love her/him. What are some things that your parents do for you? *(Let the children respond. Reflect back their answers and talk about why their parents do those things for them.)* Each of your parents does things for you because they love you and care for you. They want the best for you.

Did you know that we are all God's children, including the grownups? *(Open Bible.)* First John 3:1a says, *See what love the Father has given us, that we should be called children of God; and that is what we are.* Just like our parents, God loves us so much. God wants the best for all of us. It's good to know God loves us no matter what and forgives us when we make wrong choices. We are all God's children; that is what we are. I'm glad, and I know you are glad, too!

God Is My Shepherd

Date: Fourth Sunday of Easter

Scripture: Psalm 23

Key Verse: The Lord is my shepherd. Psalm 23:1a

Key Concepts: Trust and God's care

Materials: Bible, pictures of shepherds and biblical lands

In our Scripture lesson for today, we hear about sheep and shepherds. Let's learn about shepherds and sheep. In these pictures, you will see biblical land where shepherds watch their sheep. *(Show the pictures.)* What do you know about sheep? *(Let children respond.)* Yes, sheep say "baa," they are fluffy, and we use their wool to make clothing. We can learn more about sheep in the Bible. In 2 Samuel 12:3, Nathan tells David a story about two men who had sheep. The poor man had one little sheep that he loved "like a daughter." Sheep can be loveable creatures. Sheep aren't aggressive; they won't attack you like other animals. They need a lot of care and are helpless. They are trusting animals.

A shepherd's job was to care for the sheep. The shepherd led the sheep to the pasture to eat; provided water for them to drink; protected them from wild animals; and guided them from place to place. If a sheep was lost, a shepherd would look for it. The shepherd cared for the sheep in every possible way to keep them safe from harm.

(Open Bible.) In Psalm 23:1a, the psalmist wrote, *The LORD is my shepherd.* In the Bible, God and Jesus are sometimes described as shepherds. What do you think the psalmist meant when he wrote that God was his shepherd? *(Let the children respond.)*

God is like our shepherd because God cares for us, guides us, provides the things we need, and always looks for us if we go away from God. If we say God is our shepherd, then we trust God to care for us and to help us every day.

Words or Ways?

Date: Fourth Sunday of Easter

Scripture: 1 John 3:16-24

Key Verse: Little children, let us love, not in word or speech, but in truth and action. (1 John 3:18)

Key Concept: Loving others

Materials: Bible, posterboard, marker, white paper, index cards (optional)

Preparation: Draw a vertical line down the middle of a piece of posterboard. Write "Words" at the top of one side and "Ways" at the top of the other. Photocopy the stories printed below and cut them into individual strips, or write the names of the characters on index cards—one per card—and use those as markers for the game. Consider adding your own brief stories.

Let's play a game. *(Open Bible.)* The game is based on a verse from 1 John 3:18: *Little children, let us love, not in word or speech, but in truth and action.* This verse says that our actions show love better than our words. Instead of simply saying we love someone, we need to show that person that we love him or her. I will read stories about children. I want you to tell me whether each child shows love in words or in ways. *(Show the children the chart.)*

Joanna's Story: Joanna went to a church meeting with her mom. The meeting was about helping sick people. The speaker said one way to help the people feel better was to read them stories. Joanna knew how to read. She liked to read. She volunteered to read to people who couldn't read because of their sickness. *(Ask the children whether Joanna showed love through words or ways. Place the marker under the correct header.)*

Matt's Story: Matt met Garrett, the new boy in the neighborhood. He thought Garrett was nice. Matt even told him that he wanted him to come over and play. One day, Matt and some of his friends went to the park to play ball. As they walked toward the park, Garrett rode by on his bicycle. He was alone. Matt didn't ask Garrett to go to the park. He knew some of the other boys didn't like him. Matt said "Hi" and "How are you doing?" Then he and his friends went on to the park. At least he spoke to Garrett. *(Ask the children whether Matt showed love through words or ways. Place the marker under the correct header.)*

These simple stories help us think about how we love others. When we love people, we don't just tell them so. We act out our love in the things we do for them. Joanna knew she could read to someone who couldn't read. She showed love to another person by being with them and helping them do something they couldn't do for themselves. Matt liked Garrett, and he said hi to him as he headed toward the park with his other friends. How could Garrett show love in ways?

Jesus wants us to love others not only by saying "I love you," but also by doing things that show our love. Love brings something from inside us that makes us want to help another person, listen to a friend when they are sad, celebrate an award or a birthday, or just have a good time with someone. Love is more than a word; it's the way Jesus wants us to live with each other.

Remember the Lord

Date: Fifth Sunday of Easter Title: Remember the Lord

Scripture: Psalm 22:25-31

Key Verse: All the ends of the earth shall remember and turn to the Lord; and all the families of the nations shall worship before him. (Psalm 22:27)

Key Concepts: Praise, worship

Materials: Bible, string to tie around fingers, modern ways to remember something: planner, palm pilot, calendar

Preparation: Considering enlisting adult helpers to tie string on children's fingers, especially if you expect a large group of children.

Do you ever forget to do something you've been asked to do, such as clean your room, turn off the light, or put your clothes away? *(Let the children respond.)* Sometimes we are busy doing something else, and we forget to do what we've been told to do. Sometimes we forget to do something simply because we don't like to do it.

I tied a piece of string around my finger. Why do you think I did that? *(Let the children answer.)* Many people use computers, calendars, planners, and palm pilots to remind them of something. *(Show items to the children.)* Before these things were invented, people used to tie a string around their finger to help them remember something. My friends are here to help us. They're going to tie a string on your finger to help you remember something, too. *(Cue the adults to tie string gently on the children's fingers.)*

(Open Bible.) In Psalm 22:27, the psalmist writes, *All the ends of the earth shall remember and turn to the LORD; and all the families of the nations shall worship before him.* The psalmist knew people sometimes forget God, but he knew that one day all people would remember and worship God. We can worship God each day of the week. On certain days, we praise and honor God here in God's house. Use the string on your finger to remember that we can worship God each day with our families. We can read Scripture and pray together. We can pray just as the psalmist prayed that all the world would remember, turn, and worship God.

Fruit Gushers 1

Date: Fifth Sunday of Easter

Scripture: John 15:1-8

Key Verse: My Father is glorified by this, that you bear much fruit and become my disciples. (John 15:8)

Key Concepts: Discipleship, prayer

Materials: Bible, Fruit Gushers® candy, bowl, plant

Everyone take a piece of Fruit Gushers and eat it. *(Pass a bowl around for the children to get a piece of candy. Be sure you collect the wrappers.)* Did everyone get a piece? *(Ask one of the children directly.)* _____, what flavor was your Fruit Gusher? *(Let the child respond. He or she should mention a fruit. Ask others what flavor they had.)* When you bite the candy, what happens? *(Let the children answer.)* That's right; it squirts out juice that's the same flavor of the candy.

Have you seen a commercial for Fruit Gushers? In one commercial, when people ate the candy, their heads turned into fruit. They had heads shaped like oranges and strawberries. This was a silly commercial, but the people who make the candy wanted you to know that it tastes fruity.

Jesus talked with his disciples about being full of fruit. Jesus liked to tell stories and use symbols to explain what he meant. A symbol is something familiar that stands for something else. Jesus described himself as the vine. *(Show the children the plant.)* I brought a plant to show you. This is the vine of the plant. The vine gives the branches and the leaves everything they need to live. If I break off this branch, will it live? *(Break off part of the branch. Let the children answer.)* No, it's no longer connected to the plant.

Jesus said he was the vine and his disciples were the branches. The branches can't live away from the vine. Jesus' disciples can't live away from him. If we stay connected to Jesus through prayer, we will be fruit gushers! We will be full of the flavor of Jesus. We will be loving, joyful, peaceful, patient, kind, giving, faithful, gentle, and under control. On the commercial for Fruit Gushers, the fruit heads showed the flavor of the candy. By being full of Jesus' flavor, you will show others that you are Jesus' followers.

Earth Praise

Date: Sixth Sunday of Easter

Scripture: Psalm 98

Key Verse: Make a joyful noise to the Lord all the earth; break forth into joyous song and sing praises. (Psalm 98:4)

Key Concept: Praise

Materials: Bible, poster with the words of the "Doxology"

(Open Bible.) Psalm 98:4 says: *Make a joyful noise to the* LORD *all the earth; break forth into joyous song and sing praises.* Let's use our imaginations this morning. What do you see in your mind when you think of all the earth singing to God? *(Let the children respond.)* I see all of God's creation singing. Think about how trees, oceans, or mountains can sing praises to God. Close your eyes and picture in your mind what it would look like or sound like. *(Encourage the children to close their eyes and use their imaginations.)*

Keep your eyes closed and see if you can imagine this: You are standing by a river with a waterfall. Many rocks in the river create the waterfall. When the water falls down the slope and moves over the rocks, it makes a rushing, babbling, or trickling sound. It's a beautiful, refreshing sound that never stops. The rocks and the water are singing together. That's how they make a joyful noise to the Lord.

Do any of you have a different picture in your mind? *(Let several of the children share their description of creation praising God. Reflect back their stories.)*

In Psalm 98, the psalmist imagines the singing as the "sea roaring" and the "hills singing." Creation praises God in so many ways.

We are a part of creation. We also need to sing praises to God. Praise means worshiping or saying good things about something. Our praise belongs to God. We can praise God through songs, through the way we act, and through what we say to others.

Let's close by singing the "Doxology." It's a song that helps us praise God. This song will be our prayer together. *(Review the words with the children. Show them the poster with the printed words. Consider singing the song line by line and having the children sing each line after you. You may also invite the congregation to join you in singing.)*

Fruit Gushers 2

Date: *Sixth Sunday of Easter*

Scripture: *John 15:9-17*

Key Verses: *If you keep my commandments, you will abide in my love . . . . I have said these things to you so that my joy may be in you, and that your joy may be complete. (John 15:10a, 11)*

Key Concepts: *Discipleship—obedience and joy*

Materials: *Bible, Fruit Gushers® candy*

Last week we talked about how Jesus was like a vine. Jesus gives us life. His disciples are the branches that grow from the vine. The branches can't live apart from the vine. Jesus' disciples can't live apart from him. We learned that if we stay connected to Jesus, we will be like branches with fruit. I called us fruit gushers. *(Pass around a bowl of the Fruit Gushers and let each child take one.)*

To be fruit gushers is to be like Jesus. You are loving, joyful, peaceful, patient, kind, giving, faithful, gentle, and under control. Jesus told his disciples that one way they could stay connected is through prayer. *(Open Bible.)* In our lesson today, Jesus says, *If you keep my commandments, you will abide in my love . . . . I have said these things to you so that my joy may be in you, and that your joy may be complete.* Jesus is telling the disciples and us that to be a disciple and fruit gusher, you have to obey. Jesus told them the commandments were to love God and love others around you. He told the disciples that praying and obeying Jesus' teaching bring joy.

When you do something loving for someone else, how do you feel? *(Let children answer.)* You feel good, don't you? That's what joy is. It's more than just being happy. When we try to obey Jesus, we have a deep-down good feeling.

Soak Up Happiness

Date: Seventh Sunday of Easter

Scripture: Psalm 1

Key Verse: They are like trees planted by streams of water, which yield their fruit in its season, and their leaves do not wither. In all that they do, they prosper. (Psalm 1:3)

Key Concept: True happiness

Materials: Bible, two sponges, water, two containers for the water

Preparation: Place water in one of the containers and leave the other container empty.

Let's experiment with sponges and water. Why do we use sponges? *(Let the children answer.)* In this pan, we don't have any water. If I put the sponge in this pan, what will happen? *(Let the children respond as you place the sponge in the container.)* Nothing happens to the sponge if you place it in a pan with no water. There isn't anything for the sponge to soak up in this container.

What will happen if I place the sponge in the container of water? *(Place the sponge in the container with water and let the children respond.)* When we place this sponge in the water, it soaks up some of the water and gets wet. If we leave it in the water, it will always stay wet.

In Psalm 1, the psalmist says people are truly happy when they belong to God and study God's word. Truly happy people are people who soak up God's word. The psalmist describes these people: *(Open Bible.) They are like trees planted by streams of water, which yield their fruit in its season, and their leaves do not wither. In all that they do, they prosper.* Trees planted by streams always have water. They grow fruit and their leaves don't dry up. The water makes the tree do what a tree does—make fruit and leaves. The roots of the tree soak up the water and keep the tree healthy.

We need God's word to teach us God's way. What have you learned through Bible stories that teach you God's ways? *(Let the children answer. Suggest familiar Bible stories with themes like love and friendship.)*

We can soak up God's word by reading the Bible and studying it at church and at home. Take time each day to read a Bible story with a parent or with a brother or sister.

That's the Truth

Date: Seventh Sunday of Easter

Scripture: John 17:6-19

Key Verse: Sanctify them in the truth; your word is truth. (John 17:17)

Key Concept: God's word, truth

Materials: Bible

Let's play a game today. I am going to tell you something. I want you to decide if what I say is true or not true. For example, you know trees have leaves. That's true. What if I said trees wear clothes? That's not true.

Let's play. *(The following is a list of possible statements. Consider making up your own.)*

Statements

I am wearing blue today.

Birds lay eggs.

Elephants are purple.

Our church has an organ.

Lions make good pets.

Jesus loves us.

The Bible is God's word for us to read and learn.

When we know for sure that something is a certain way, we say it is true. You know elephants aren't purple. You have seen an elephant or pictures of elephants, and you know they are gray. You know lions don't make good pets because they are big, wild animals. You know birds lay eggs because you have seen a bird's nest or seen pictures of a bird's eggs. You know Jesus loves us because you have learned about it at home, Sunday school, and in worship. You also know because you read stories from the Bible, which is God's word for us to read and learn.

(Open Bible.) In John 17:17, Jesus prays for his disciples. He says, *Sanctify them in the truth; your word is truth. Sanctify* is a big word. It means to set something apart as holy or special. Jesus prayed that his disciples would be holy and full of truth that comes from God's word. We can also become holy and fill ourselves with the truth from God's word.

Help Us Pray

Date: Pentecost

Scripture: Romans 8:22-27

Key Verse: Likewise the Spirit helps us in our weakness; for we do not know how to pray as we ought, but that very Spirit intercedes with sighs too deep for words. (Romans 8:26)

Key Concepts: Holy Spirit, prayer

Materials: Bible, card stock, scissors, markers

Preparation: Make bookmarks from card stock with these words: "The Holy Spirit helps me pray when I don't know what to say.—Romans 8:26"

Today is Pentecost. We celebrate the coming of the Holy Spirit to Christians. Jesus told his disciples that he would send the Holy Spirit to guide and teach all Christians. The Holy Spirit helps us in many ways. One way is when we pray. What do you pray for? *(Let the children answer, reflecting back their responses.)* We pray for many things—our families, our church, our schools, our neighborhoods, our country, and our world.

Have you ever wanted to pray but didn't know what to say? *(Let the children respond.)* Sometimes it's hard to pray when we are sad. When a friend is sick or when a pet dies, we feel sad. If someone asked you to say something and you felt very sad, you might sigh. *(Exaggerate a sigh.)* Sometimes we're not sure what to say, even though we have strong feelings inside.

(Open Bible.) In Romans 8:26, Paul tells us that the Holy Spirit can pray for us when we don't know what to say. It says, *Likewise the Spirit helps us in our weakness; for we do not know how to pray as we ought, but that very Spirit intercedes with sighs too deep for words.* The word *intercede* means to ask something for someone else. I would intercede for you if I asked your parent if you could go to the park. When we don't know what to say to God, the Spirit says it for us with sighs that speak of our deepest feelings to God.

I want to give you each a bookmark to remind you that the Holy Spirit can help you pray. It says, "The Holy Spirit helps me pray when I don't know what to say." Remember that Jesus sent the Holy Spirit to teach us and help us make choices that are pleasing to him.

Common Lectionary
Year C

Protector of the Faithful

Date: First Sunday in Lent

Scripture: Psalm 91

Key Verses: Those who love me, I will deliver; I will protect those who know my name. When they call to me, I will answer them; I will be with them in trouble, I will rescue them and honor them. (Psalm 91:14-15)

Key Concept: God's protection

Materials: Bible, pictures of a doctor, police officer, and firefighter (include male and female workers)

Let's look at these pictures. Who is in this picture? *(Hold up the picture of the police officer. Let the children respond.)* What does a police officer do for us? *(Let the children answer. Guide them to talk about how police officers protect us.)* Police officers help us to be safe. They protect us from people who might hurt us.

Who is in this picture? *(Show the picture and let children reply.)* How does a firefighter help us? *(Let the children respond.)* Firefighters put out fires. They teach us fire safety rules so we can prevent fires and know how to be safe in case of a fire.

Who is in this picture? *(Show the picture and let the children respond.)* How do doctors help us? *(Let the children answer.)* Doctors can help us when we're sick. They also protect us from getting diseases by giving us shots to keep us from getting sick. Doctors make sure we're growing like we should and that we eat right so we can be healthy and strong.

All of these helpers protect us and help keep us safe. We're thankful we have them in our community.

We have another big protector and helper. Can you guess who that is? *(Let the children answer.)* You're right—God is our protector and helper. We all believe in God. We love and trust God. So did the psalmist who wrote Psalm 91. *(Open Bible.)* Verses 14-15 say, *Those who love me, I will deliver; I will protect those who know my name. When they call to me, I will answer them; I will be with them in trouble, I will rescue them and honor them.*

The psalm writer knew God listened and answered prayers. Isn't it good to know that God will listen and answer prayer? God will be with us and help us when we find ourselves in trouble. God is with us and helps us all. the time.

God's Powerful Word

Date: First Sunday in Lent

Scripture: Luke 4:1-13

Key Verses: Jesus answered him, "It is written, 'One does not live by bread alone.'" ...Jesus answered him, "It is written, 'Worship the Lord your God, and serve only him.'" ...Jesus answered him, "It is said, 'Do not put the Lord your God to the test.'" (Luke 4:4, 8, 12)

Key Concepts: Power of God's word, temptation

Materials: Bible

This is the first Sunday in the church season we call Lent. Lent lasts for forty days before Easter, not including Sundays. During Lent, we get ready for Easter. We think about what it means to follow Jesus and to know and love him more. We try to understand Jesus' ways even more than before. One of the ways we can learn what it means to be more like Jesus is to read God's word—the Bible.

Lent lasts forty days. In our Gospel lesson, Jesus is in the desert for forty days. The devil tries to get Jesus to do wrong things. Let's explore what Jesus did when the devil tempted him.

Do you know what it means to be tempted? *(Let the children answer.)* When we're tempted, someone tries to get us to do something we know is wrong. Maybe you have been tempted to take the last piece of candy that was for your brother or sister. You know it's wrong, but you take it anyway. Maybe your schoolmates try to get you to say cruel things to another classmate. That's wrong, too. As you get older, you will make more and more choices. We all need a way to make the right choice when we're tempted. Jesus can help us do this.

When Jesus was tempted with right or wrong choices in the desert, he answered the devil with Scripture—God's word. *(Open Bible.)* First, the devil tempted Jesus with food. Jesus hadn't eaten during his days in the desert. He was hungry, but he answered the devil this way: *"It is written, 'One does not live by bread alone.'"* This verse is also found in Deuteronomy 8:3. Next, the devil tempted Jesus by telling him he could rule the world if he worshiped the devil. Jesus answered the temptation with Scripture from Deuteronomy 6:13: *"It is written, 'Worship the Lord your God, and serve only him.'"* For his last temptation, the devil used Scripture. He said that the angels would keep Jesus safe if he jumped from the top of the temple building. Again, Jesus answered him with Scripture from Deuteronomy 6:16: *"It is said, 'Do not put the Lord your God to the test.'"*

In church and at home, we learn Scripture. Scripture can help us when we are tempted and have to choose between right and wrong. If someone asked you to steal something, can you think of a verse that could help you make the right choice? *(Let the children respond. Lead them to think of stories they know and particularly the Ten Commandments. Open Bible to Exodus.)* Exodus 20:15 says, *You shall not steal.* Take time during this season of Lent to learn Scripture verses and stories of Jesus that can help you make right choices when you are tempted.

Everyday Trusting

Date: Second Sunday in Lent

Scripture: Genesis 15:1-12, 17-18

Key Verse: And [Abraham] believed the Lord; and the Lord reckoned it to him as righteousness. (Genesis 15:6)

Key Concept: Trusting God with everyday matters

Materials: Bible, family picture that includes children, picture of a house with a yard

Preparation: You may want to use pictures of some of the children's families. Either ask parents in advance, or bring a pictorial directory of church members.

Let's look at these pictures. Who is in this picture? *(Show the family picture that includes children. It could be your family, a family in your church, or a picture from a magazine. Let the children respond.)* It's a picture of a family. All of us are a part of a family. Can you name some of the things your family does each day? *(Let the children answer. Expect a variety of answers such as eating, dressing, going to school, day care, etc.)* Our days as a family are full of all kinds of activities.

I have another picture I want to show you. What is in this picture? *(Show the picture of a house with a yard. Let the children respond.)* This is a picture of a house and yard. *(Note: Adjust the following to fit the children in your congregation. Include all types of homes.)* All of us have a house and a yard where we live and play. This is part of our everyday life. It has all our "stuff," and it's the place we gather with our family.

In our Old Testament reading, Abraham didn't have a family with children. He left his home and his yard when God told him to leave. Abraham must have trusted God with everyday things. God came to Abraham in a dream and told him he would have children and his family would be as many as the stars in the sky. *(Open Bible.)* Genesis 15:6 says, *And [Abraham] believed the Lord; and the Lord reckoned it to him as righteousness.* People were called "righteous" if they loved God and did things that pleased God. Abraham loved and pleased God. God also told Abraham he would have land that would belong to his children. Abraham believed and trusted what God told him. He tried to please God by letting God help him with everyday things such as his family and his home.

We can let God help us with all the activities of our days. How can we trust God to help us every day? *(Let the children respond.)* We can let God help us with our friends, what we say, and how we play together. There are so many things that we can't name them all. Let's remember that we can trust God to help us with everyday things, big or small.

Stand Firm

Date: Second Sunday in Lent

Scripture: Philippians 3:17–4:1

Key Verse: Therefore, my brothers and sisters, whom I love and long for, my joy and crown, stand firm in the Lord in this way, my beloved. (Philippians 4:1)

Key Concept: Following Jesus' example

Materials: Bible

I need volunteers to help me. *(Choose several children for the following activities.)* I want _____ to walk to the wall and try to push it down. *(The children will probably laugh and question your request, but insist that the child try to knock it down.)* Okay, the wall is too strong to knock down. I want _____ to try to push over the front pew. *(Only do this if the pews are bolted securely to the floor.)* It looks like we can't move the walls or the pew. We might say the walls and the pew are firm. This means they are solid and secure. It would be hard to push through them.

In the New Testament, Paul, who was a follower of Jesus, wrote letters to Christians to let them know how to follow Jesus. *(Open Bible.)* In a letter called Philippians, Paul wrote, *Therefore, my brothers and sisters, whom I love and long for, my joy and crown, stand firm in the Lord in this way, my beloved.* Paul told these Christians to "stand firm" in the Lord. What do you think he meant by that? *(Let the children respond.)* Paul taught the Christians that they were to follow Jesus' example. They weren't supposed to let other ideas or teachings get in the way. Paul was telling them to be firm like that wall. It shouldn't be easy for someone to push them away from following Jesus' example.

We can "stand firm," too. Can you think of a time when you made the right choice because of your belief in Jesus? *(Let the children answer. Provide an example if necessary, such as following Jesus by being nice to someone instead of joining others in being mean to him or her.)* We can stand firm by following Jesus' example.

Seek and Call on the Lord

Date: Third Sunday in Lent

Scripture: Isaiah 55:1-9

Key Verse: Seek the Lord while he may be found, call upon him while he is near . . . . (Isaiah 55:6)

Key Concepts: God's presence, prayer

Materials: Bible, magnifying glass(es), small cards, tape

Preparation: Print the following clues on small cards. Write small so the children need to use the magnifying glass to read them. Clue #1: It's bigger than you can imagine. Clue #2 can be found under the first pew. Clue #2: You can call, but not on the phone. Clue #3 can be found taped to the pulpit. Clue #3: Can be found anywhere and is always near.

Good detectives will help me this morning. A good detective needs a magnifying glass. I need three volunteers to be our chief detectives. *(Choose children who can read the clues.)* Here is the first clue. _____, I would like for you to read this clue. *(Let the child read the first clue with the magnifying glass.)* _____, go find the next clue under the pew and bring it here to read. *(Let the child retrieve the clue and read it with the magnifying glass.)* Let's find our last clue and see if we can figure out what we are looking for. _____, go and get our last clue from the pulpit and bring it here to read to us. *(Let the child get the clue and read it for the group.)* Can you guess who we are looking for? *(Review the clues and let the children respond.)* Yes, we're looking for God.

(Open Bible.) Isaiah 55:6 says, *Seek the LORD while he may be found, call upon him while he is near.* How can we seek and call God? *(Let the children respond. Accept their answers and guide them to think of ways they acknowledge God's presence.)* When we come to church to worship, we're seeking or looking for God. We come to praise God, and we know God is with us. In our worship time, we have a prayer called an invocation. In this prayer, we ask God to be with us as we worship and praise God. We call on God through prayer. We don't have to be at church to seek or call God. We can do that anywhere, because God is everywhere. God is with us in everything we do and everywhere we go. We can call to God through prayer anytime.

Whose Sin Is Worse?

Date: Third Sunday in Lent

Scripture: Luke 13:1-9

Key Verse: "No, I tell you; but unless you repent, you will all perish just as they did." (Luke 13:5)

Key Concepts: Sin, repentance

Materials: Bible

Do you know what sin is? *(Let the children respond.)* Sin is when we do something that separates us from God and God's ways. Can you name some sins? *(Let the children answer. Depending on their maturity, you may want to guide them to consider various sins such as lying, cheating, stealing, etc.)* We have named things that are not pleasing to God. Which sin do you think is the worst? *(Let the children respond. It is likely they will choose what most people see as the greater offense.)* Let's look at Scripture to see what Jesus said about sin.

(Open Bible.) Our lesson is from Luke 13. In this story, people ask Jesus if certain Galileans suffered and died because they were worse sinners than other Galileans. During that time, people believed that bad things and suffering happened because of sin. Jesus answered their question by telling them sin is sin, no matter what someone does wrong. He tried to tell them all people are sinners, and all people need to turn away from sin and turn back to God. Turning away from sin and turning back to God is called *repentance*. In Luke 13:5, Jesus says, *"No, I tell you; but unless you repent, you will all perish just as they did."*

Jesus then tells a story, called a parable, about repentance. A person had a fig tree that had not produced fruit for three years. The owner wanted to cut it down, but the gardener asked the owner to let it live for one more year. The gardener wanted to care for the tree and see if he could help turn it around to produce fruit. Remember that *repentance* means to turn around—to change completely. Jesus was trying to teach the people that everyone needs to turn from the wrong things in their lives.

During this season of Lent, Jesus wants us to turn around—to change completely. Jesus wants us to repent and turn away from our sin. This is something we must do each and every day.

Where Would We Find Jesus?

Date: Fourth Sunday in Lent

Scripture: Luke 15:1-3, 11b-32

Key Verses: Now all the tax collectors and sinners were coming near to listen to him. And the Pharisees and the scribes were grumbling and saying, "This fellow welcomes sinners and eats with them." (Luke 15:1-2)

Key Concept: God's inclusiveness

Materials: Bible, stuffed sheep (optional)

Let's use our imaginations today. If Jesus were here in our town/city, where do you think he would go to eat? Where do you think he would live? *(Let the children respond. Guide them to think about where Jesus went in the Bible stories they know. Consider suggesting one or two places where the children wouldn't choose to go, but use care with your examples.)*

When Jesus was here on earth, many religious leaders complained. Jesus was a friend to people they considered sinners. *(Open Bible.)* Luke 15:1-2 says, *Now all the tax collectors and sinners were coming near to listen to him. And the Pharisees and the scribes were grumbling and saying, "This fellow welcomes sinners and eats with them."* Jesus was with the "outsiders." The church leaders thought no one should be with these kinds of people. The leaders, called Pharisees and scribes, grumbled to Jesus because he included everyone as his friend. Jesus told them a story, or parable, about a lost sheep. *(Show a stuffed sheep to the children. Tell the parable in your own words using the story below as a guide. As a listening cue, you might have the children make sheep sounds every time you say the word "sheep." If you do, pause after the word and continue once the children are quiet.)*

Parable

Pretend you are a shepherd and you have 100 sheep. You love all your sheep, and you take good care of them. Every night you take them back to the pen. You count the sheep to make sure all of them are there. One night, you count your sheep and there are only ninety-nine. The other sheep must be lost. It's only one little sheep. You still have ninety-nine sheep in the pen.

What would you do? *(Let the children respond.)* You would look for the lost sheep.

You look for the sheep and find it. Then you tell your friends because you are so happy. Jesus said God is like the shepherd, and God loves all people. God wants all people to come and worship God. God cares about even one person who does not know God.

The parable teaches us that God cares about all people. God loves everyone, even the people we may not like. Have you ever left out boys or girls because they wear strange clothes, look different, or act in ways that seem odd? *(Let the children answer.)* We all leave out people sometimes. Our reasons for doing this are usually not very good. Jesus wants us to include people who get left out and love them just as he would.

Christ's Ambassadors

Date: Fourth Sunday in Lent

Scripture: 2 Corinthians 5:16-21

Key Verse: So we are ambassadors for Christ, since God is making his appeal through us . . . . (2 Corinthians 5:20a)

Key Concept: Telling others about Christ

Materials: Bible; sticky labels or card stock and tape, marker (optional)

Preparation: If you choose, create badges to give the children. Using a marker, print "Ambassador for Jesus" on sticky labels or on card stock.

Does your mom or dad or another adult ever watch the news? Have you heard the word *ambassador* on the news? *(Let the children respond.)* An ambassador is a person that is chosen to take a message to other people. Our country sends different people to other countries to be messengers. They talk about how our countries can work together. An ambassador is a messenger who does a special job for us.

Do you think you can be an ambassador? *(Let the children respond.)* If we love Jesus and trust in him, we are ambassadors or messengers for Jesus. *(Open Bible.)* Paul wrote a letter to Christians in the city of Corinth. He wrote, *So we are ambassadors for Christ, since God is making his appeal through us.* Let's say this verse in different words so it will be easier to understand—We are messengers for Jesus, since God is making God's message known to others through us. Each day we need to remember that what we do and say is our message to others. If we are Jesus' messengers, then the things we do and say should be things Jesus would do or say. Can you think of ways you could be Jesus' messenger? *(Let the children answer. Use their answers to conclude the sermon. If you choose, give out the badges you created and encourage the children to wear them and share Jesus with others.)* Here is a reminder that you're ambassadors for Jesus. You can serve him, too.

What Did You Expect?

Date: Fifth Sunday in Lent

Scripture: Isaiah 43:16-21

Key Verses: Do not remember the former things, or consider the things of old. I am about to do a new thing. (Isaiah 43:18-19a)

Key Concept: Grace

Materials: Bible

Have your parents ever made you go somewhere you didn't want to go, but you were surprised by how much fun you had there? *(Let the children respond.)* Sometimes things turn out better than we expect. *Expect* means look forward to something that will happen. My son asked for one Care Bear for his birthday. When he opened his presents, he got four Care Bears! He was excited, and he got more than he expected.

(Open Bible.) In Isaiah, the prophet tells God's chosen people, the Israelites, *Do not remember the former things, or consider the things of old. I am about to do a new thing.* This was God's message to God's people. Expect bigger things than what you have already seen and heard.

Let's remember stories about Moses. Moses helped God's people get out of Egypt. They were slaves to Pharaoh and worked hard for the Egyptians. God helped Moses get God's people, the Israelites, out of Egypt. This was called the exodus. When the people left Egypt, they crossed the Red Sea. God pushed back the water so they could cross on dry land. Then Moses led the people in the desert, and God provided them with food and water. They headed for a land where they could plant good crops and raise their animals. This land was called the promised land. The Israelites celebrated the exodus as God's great power and victory. They didn't realize that God would do something greater than that. They didn't expect God's grace. They didn't think about the new things God wanted for them and wanted to give them.

The word *grace* is hard to describe. Grace is love that God has for us. Grace is kindness and favor God shows us. It's love that we don't earn. We don't have to do anything to deserve God's love. God just loves us. In Ephesians 2:8, Paul describes grace as a gift of God. *(Read the verse.)*

God gave us a wonderful gift. Can you think of something God has given to you because God loves you? *(Let the children respond. You may need to guide them to think about creation, parents, teachers, homes, food, etc.)* Out of kindness, God has given us so much. We are thankful for all God has done. We show our thankfulness by praying and by helping others. We can always expect God's grace. It never runs out, and sometimes it can surprise us more than we could ever imagine.

Full of Love

Date: *Fifth Sunday in Lent*

Scripture: *John 12:1-8*

Key Verse: *"You always have the poor with you, but you do not always have me." (John 12:8)*

Key Concept: *Love*

Materials: *Bible, bottle of vanilla extract*

Our New Testament story is from the Gospel of John. *(Open your Bible.)* This story happened just before Palm Sunday, when Jesus went to Jerusalem.

Jesus and his disciples came to Bethany, a town outside Jerusalem. They stayed with Jesus' close friends Lazarus, Martha, and Mary. Lazarus, Martha, and Mary threw Jesus a big dinner party. Martha served the dinner while Lazarus sat with Jesus and the disciples and talked. While they were talking, Mary came into the room with a bottle of perfume. *(Open a bottle of vanilla extract to serve as perfume.)* She opened the expensive bottle of perfume and rubbed it on Jesus' feet with her hair. *(Rub a dab of vanilla extract on some of the children's wrists.)* The smell of the perfume filled the house. *(Let all the children smell the vanilla extract.)*

Judas, one of the disciples, smelled the perfume. He looked at Jesus and asked why the perfume wasn't sold and given to the poor. It could have been sold for 300 denarii, which was a whole year's pay for some workers. Judas acted like he cared for the poor. Jesus knew differently, though. Jesus told Judas to leave her alone.

Mary loved Jesus very much. Jesus reminded Judas and the other disciples by saying this: *"You always have the poor with you, but you do not always have me."* Jesus was trying to tell the disciples that his time on earth was coming to an end. Jesus wanted them to know that there would always be poor people to care for, but Mary's love of Jesus was the kind of love that wouldn't forget the poor. Mary was generous to Jesus, and she would act that way toward others.

Smell the sweet perfume and remember the generous love Mary had for Jesus. I want to leave you and the grownups with a question to think about. Do we love like Mary loved?

Speaking Stones

Date: Sixth Sunday in Lent (Palm Sunday)

Scripture: Luke 19:28-40

Key Verses: Some of the Pharisees in the crowd said to him, "Teacher, order your disciples to stop." He answered, "I tell you, if these were silent, the stones would shout out." (Luke 19:39-40)

Key Concept: Praise

Materials: Bible, small polished stone for each child

(As the children come forward, hand each of them a stone. Guide them to sit down after they receive one.) I gave each of you a stone. I want you to feel it. Move it around in your hand. Now I put it next to your ear and listen to it. *(As you give these instructions, rub a stone and put it to your ear.)* Did your stone say anything? *(Let the children respond. They may laugh about this.)*

We call today Palm Sunday. *(Open Bible.)* In Luke, the Palm Sunday story is in chapter 19. Jesus was on his way to Jerusalem. He sent some of his disciples ahead. He told them to find a colt for him to ride. When they brought the colt back, the disciples placed their coats (or cloaks) on the colt. Jesus sat on the colt. As he came down the road, people began to spread their coats on the ground in front of him. As he got closer to Jerusalem, many of Jesus' disciples began praising God in loud voices. They yelled, *"Blessed is the king who comes in the name of the Lord!"* (v. 38).

Some of the Pharisees didn't like what the disciples said. The Pharisees were preachers who believed people had to follow many rules to please God. They didn't like some of the things Jesus did and said. Some of them didn't believe he was God's Son. Luke 19:39-40 says, *Some of the Pharisees in the crowd said to him, "Teacher, order your disciples to stop." He answered, "I tell you, if these were silent, the stones would shout out."*

Look at your stone. What do you think it would have been like if the stones started shouting? *(Let the children respond.)* What do you think the stones would have shouted as Jesus passed by? *(Let the children answer.)*

Keep your stone by your bed as a reminder to praise Jesus. Jesus showed us so much about how we are to live together and love each other. Jesus comes today as our king, and we will praise him and thank him.

We Are Witnesses

Date: Easter Sunday Title: We Are Witnesses

Scripture: Acts 10:34-43

Key Verses: *We are witnesses to all that he did both in Judea and in Jerusalem. They put him to death by hanging him on a tree; but God raised him on the third day and allowed him to appear. (Acts 10:39-40)*

Key Concepts: Easter, meaning of witness

Materials: Bible

Happy Easter! Today is the most important Christian holiday that we celebrate. It should be an exciting day for us. Jesus is alive! That's our exciting news.

What have you seen with your eyes that excited you? *(Let the children respond. Expect a variety of answers. Repeat the children's answers as a way to explain witnessing something. For example, a child may have seen [witnessed] a car race in which his/her favorite driver won. Guide them to understand witness as seeing something and then telling about it.)*

In our reading from Acts 10, Peter tells the exciting story of Jesus to the Gentiles. Gentiles were people who weren't Jews. The Jews were God's chosen people from Old Testament times. In a few verses, Peter tells the story of Jesus to the Gentiles gathered at Cornelius's house He starts with John the Baptist and goes through the story of Jesus. *(Open Bible.)* This is what he told those who listened: *We are witnesses to all that [Jesus] did both in Judea and Jerusalem. They put him to death by hanging him on a tree; but God raised him on the third day and allowed him to appear.* Peter and the disciples saw Jesus in action. They saw him feed a lot of people with small amounts of food. They saw Jesus healing the sick. They saw him die on the cross. They saw him again after God raised him from death. Peter and the disciples saw or witnessed all of these events, and now they had to tell others about it. They began to tell the story of Jesus to everyone who would listen.

We didn't get to see Jesus when he was here on earth. That was a long time ago. We do have stories of Jesus we read in our Bibles. The Bible tells us what Jesus did and who he was. Through the stories, we can learn how Jesus lived and how he taught his disciples to follow God's way. We can see people today who live by Jesus' example. We can see that they are followers of Jesus by what they do and say.

As each of you grow and get bigger and bigger, you will be able to tell what you've seen and learned about Jesus. You can all tell something you know about Jesus from what you have already learned. You can continue to witness or see and tell as you learn more about Jesus. Today, we can all tell others the exciting story that Jesus is alive!

Musical Praise

Date: Second Sunday of Easter

Scripture: Psalm 150

Key Verse: Let everything that breathes praise the Lord! Praise the Lord! (Psalm 150:6)

Key Concept: Praise

Materials: Bible, instruments named in the Scripture

Preparation: If possible, find children, youth, or adults who play instruments such as trumpet, harp, tambourine, string instruments, cymbals, etc. Consider having these instrumentalists play something together during your time with the children, such as the "Doxology." Another option is to use a keyboard with settings that sound like various instruments.

This is our first time together after Easter. Since Easter is such a great celebration, we continue celebrating today. I've invited friends to play instruments for us. *(At this point have the people you recruited play the "Doxology" or another familiar praise song for the children.)* Each of these instruments played a song of praise. Every time we come together to worship, we sing and play songs to praise God. Our friends played what we call the "Doxology." The word *doxology* is a religious word that means praise.

(Open Bible.) Psalm 150 is a doxology—a hymn of praise. It tells us how we can praise with music. It speaks of praising God with trumpets, harps, lutes, tambourines, stringed instruments, pipe instruments, cymbals, and even with our bodies by dancing. *(Optional: You could play the praise song and let the children dance.)* The last verse of the psalm says, *Let everything that breathes praise the LORD! Praise the LORD!* What is everything that breathes? *(Let the children respond. They may think of every kind of creature. Encourage them to use their imaginations to tell you how some of the animals might praise God.)* It means all creatures can praise the Lord. It means we're asked to praise God, too. How can we do that? *(Let the children answer, and affirm their suggestions.)* There are so many ways we can praise the Lord. Celebrating Easter gives us a chance to praise God. We can celebrate a God who loves us so much. Let's continue to worship and praise the Lord!

Easter Every Day

Date: Second Sunday of Easter

Scripture: Acts 5:27-32 (33-42)

Key Verse: And every day in the temple and at home they did not cease to teach and proclaim Jesus as the Messiah. (Acts 5:42)

Key Concept: Discipleship

Materials: Bible, plastic eggs, stickers of Christian symbols or permanent markers

Preparation: If you do not have stickers of Christian symbols for the children to use, draw Christian symbols on the eggs with a permanent marker. Prepare one for each child.

Did you know that Christians celebrate something every day? Do you know what it is? *(Let the children respond. Accept the children's answers. Then guide the next part of the sermon depending on what they say.)* We call ourselves Christians because we follow Jesus. We follow Jesus because we believe he is God's Son and our Savior. We believe Jesus died on the cross to forgive our sins. We believe Jesus came back to life—this is called resurrection—and promised us that if we follow him, we can live with him forever. We celebrate Jesus' resurrection especially on Easter, but every day should be Easter for us.

This was the way Peter and other close followers of Jesus, or apostles, acted. *(Open Bible.)* In Acts 5, Peter and the apostles are arrested because they preach and teach the Easter story of Jesus. Peter and the apostles were brought before the council of the high priests. They had to answer questions about what they preached and taught. Peter told the priests what he believed and preached. The religious leaders got so mad that they wanted to kill Peter and the apostles.

One Pharisee, named Gamaliel, was respected. The other priests listened to him. Gamaliel sent Peter and the apostles out of the room so he could talk with the council. Gamaliel told the others to leave the aspostles alone. He told them that if what Peter and the apostles said weren't from God, it would fail. If they were from God, the religious leaders might find themselves fighting against God. The council let Peter and the apostles go. Acts 5:42 says, *And every day in the temple and at home they did not cease to teach and proclaim Jesus as the Messiah.* Peter and the apostles celebrated and taught the Easter story every day.

Please take a plastic egg and stickers to create a reminder of Easter. *(Adapt this activity if you do not use stickers.)* As followers of Jesus, we're to celebrate Easter every day. It should happen naturally. We should never stop teaching and telling others that Jesus is our Messiah, which means the one who saves us from our sins. That doesn't mean we have to use words all the time. If we live Jesus' way, our actions show others that we celebrate Easter.

Instruments of Change

Date: *Third Sunday of Easter*

Scripture: *Acts 9:1-6 (7-20)*

Key Verse: *But the Lord said to him, "Go, for he is an instrument whom I have chosen to bring my name before Gentiles and kings and before the people of Israel. (Acts 9:15)*

Key Concept: *Discipleship*

Materials: *Bible, barometer or other instruments that measure change*

Have you ever changed your mind about something? *(Let the children respond. Provide an example if necessary.)* We can change our minds about many things.

I brought a barometer with me. Do you know how this instrument, or tool, is used? *(Let the children answer if they know.)* A barometer helps measure the change in air pressure. It helps a weather forecaster tell what the weather will be like. When the air pressure is lower, there is rain or snow. When the pressure is higher, we have nice, sunny weather. *(Discuss what the barometer reading is for today.)* We call a barometer an instrument or tool because it helps us see how the air pressure changes. Have you ever thought about how we can be tools or instruments of change?

Paul found out he could change. Before Paul became a follower of Jesus, he tried to get rid of all the Christians. He was on his way to Damascus when a light blinded him and Jesus spoke to him. Paul went to Damascus and waited on Jesus' messenger to come. This messenger's name was Ananias. *(Open Bible.)* In Acts 9:15, God speaks to Ananias about Paul. *But the Lord said to him, "Go, for he is an instrument whom I have chosen to bring my name before Gentiles and kings and before the people of Israel."* Paul changed from a man who wanted to kill Christians to a man who went everywhere telling others about Jesus. He changed inside. He became God's tool or instrument to tell others about Jesus.

Paul changed in a big way. As you continue to learn more about what it means to follow Christ, you will change inside, too. You are already God's tools or instruments by being here as a part of our church family. We learn from you how God wants us to change. We all help each other discover how God wants us to learn and change. We just have to watch and listen.

Gone Fishing

Date: Third Sunday of Easter

Scripture: John 21:1-19

Key Verses: Jesus said to them, "Children, you have no fish, have you?" They answered him, "No." He said to them, "Cast the net to the right side of the boat, and you will find some." So they cast it, and now they were not able to haul it in because there were so many fish. (John 21:5-6)

Key Concept: Recognizing Jesus

Materials: Bible, fishing net, seashells (optional)

Preparation: As you tell the story, guide the children in motions to act it out. Ask an adult volunteer to say the words of Jesus from the back of the sanctuary. Also ask two older children to play the part of the disciple who says, "It's Jesus!" and the part of Peter.

It was a sunny, hot day along the Sea of Tiberias. *(Wipe your forehead, squint in the sunlight, and fan yourself with your hands.)* Can you feel the heat and hear the waves against the shore? *(Put your hand to your ear.)*

We are a group of Jesus' disciples. We sat on the beach and talked to each other about many things. We sat around most of the day. When night came, Simon Peter stood up and said, "I'm going fishing." *(Have a child stand up and say, "I'm going fishing.")* The rest of us decided to go with him. We said, "We want to go, too!" *(Encourage the children to join in.)* We got in the boat and rowed. *(Pretend you are holding an oar and row.)* When we got to a good spot, we stopped. We threw out the nets. *(Toss the net you brought. Or pretend you are tossing a net.)* Then we pulled it in. *(Make a motion of pulling in the net. Continue making these motions as you try to catch fish.)* No fish. We threw out the net again. We pulled it in. No fish. We threw out the net again. We pulled it in. No fish.

We did this all night long. My arms are so tired now! *(Shake your arms.)* We are all getting hungry, but there are no fish to eat. *(Rub your stomach.)*

Look, the sun is beginning to come up. *(Put your hand up over your eyes and look up.)*

(Have an adult at the back of the church say Jesus' words: "Children, you have no fish, do you?") There's a man standing on the shore. He's right. We

have no fish. *(Yell the following toward the back of the church)* No! We didn't catch anything!

(Have the adult say Jesus' words: "Cast your net to the right side of the boat, and you will find some.") Did you hear what he said? Well, I guess we should try. Let's throw our net out again. *(Make the motion. When you bring the net up, act as if it is too heavy to lift. Encourage the children to help you with it.)* Wow! Look at all of these fish!

(Have a child say, "It's Jesus!") Did she say it's Jesus? *(Have a child pretend to jump from the boat and "swim" to Jesus.)* Oh, look at Peter! He's so excited that he's swimming to the shore! Let's haul this net to the shore so we can see Jesus, too. *(Get the rest of the children to help you pull the full net to shore.)*

What a trip we just had! We got to see Jesus. That's how it was for Jesus' disciples. Jesus appeared to them. At first they didn't know who it was. They listened and did what he asked them to do. They caught a lot of fish, but they also knew this man was Jesus. Sometimes when we listen and follow what we are taught about Jesus, we know him better, too. As you continue to grow and learn, you will know Jesus more and more. As I get older and listen and learn, I know Jesus more and more. It's something we do all of our lives. Let's live each day as Jesus' followers or disciples.

What Do You Want?

Date: Fourth Sunday of Easter

Scripture: Psalm 23

Key Verse: The Lord is my shepherd, I shall not want. (Psalm 23:1)

Key Concept: Trust

Materials: Bible, brown paper lunch bag for each child

Everyone please take a bag. *(Let the children get a bag and sit.)* Let's use our imaginations. Your bag is a magic bag, and you can reach in and get anything you want. Open your bag and look inside. Can you picture what you want? It can be any size, shape, or color. It could be anything you want.

(Let each child share what he or she sees in the magic bag. Limit their sharing to one or two things. Then share what you see in your magic bag. Expect a variety of answers from the children.)

We want many things. Have you ever thought about the difference between the things we want and the things we need? The things we need are things we must have. We must have water to live. Our bodies can't work without it. We must have food. Our bodies can't work well without it. We must have a place to live to keep us dry.

(Open Bible.) David wrote Psalm 23. He thought about wants and needs. He wrote, *The LORD is my shepherd, I shall not want.* David knew that one of his needs was to trust God to provide for him. We can trust God to care for us and give us what we need, because God loves us so much.

All God's People

Date: Fourth Sunday of Easter

Scripture: Revelation 7:9-17

Key Verse: After this I looked, and there was a great multitude that no one could count, from every nation, from all tribes and peoples and languages, standing before the throne and before the Lamb, robed in white, with palm branches in their hands. (Revelation 7:9)

Key Concept: Diversity and unity of God's people

Materials: Bible, words for "Jesus Loves the Little Children," palm branches, costumes (optional)

Preparation: Recruit youth or adult volunteers to say, "Praise God" in various languages. If possible, include people who represent various ethnic groups. Ask these volunteers to wear white robes or dress in white.

Do you know the song "Jesus Loves the Little Children"? *(Sing the song for the children. Ask those who know it to help you teach the rest of the children.)* Let's sing it again, and you can try to sing along. *(Sing the song again.)* That's one of my favorite songs. It tells me Jesus loves everybody everywhere. It doesn't matter what color their skin is or where they live—Jesus loves all the children of the world.

The Bible has a verse about the people who will be a part of God's kingdom. Jesus promised he would come back one day. When he comes back, our world will be different. There will be peace, and people will not fight anymore. There will be no more sickness. There will be no hunger. All people will have enough of everything good. All people will praise God. That's what God's kingdom will be like.

(Have your volunteers begin saying "Praise God" in the various languages. Cue them to come forward in their white costumes carrying palm branches. Open your Bible.) Revelation 7:9 describes people in God's kingdom. It says, *After this I looked, and there was a great multitude that no one could count, from every nation, from all tribes and peoples and languages, standing before the throne and before the Lamb, robed in white, with palm branches in their hands.* The book of Revelation gives us a picture of all kinds of people praising God. They speak many different languages. There are too many to

count! Even though these people are different, they all sing the same song of praise to Jesus. It's a beautiful picture.

Jesus hasn't come yet, but we can sing a song of praise to Jesus. We can know that people all over the world are praising Jesus today. We are part of a large number of people all around the world who want to praise Jesus. *(If your congregation recites the Apostle's Creed, consider explaining the holy catholic church at this time. Others may want to talk about our larger church family that includes all people who proclaim that Jesus is Lord.)*

Free Spirit

Date: Fifth Sunday of Easter

Scripture: Acts 11:1-18

Key Verse: If then God gave them the same gift [of the Holy Spirit] that he gave us when we believed in the Lord Jesus Christ, who was I that I could hinder God? (Acts 11:17)

Key Concept: Holy Spirit

Materials: Bible, small sheet or blanket, stuffed animals or plastic figures to represent the animals in Peter's dream

Sometimes we describe other people as being "free spirits." Free-spirited people don't always go by the rules. They like to try new things. They're creative, and they question everything. They don't always do things the way they've always been done. For example, when my brother-in-law was little he liked to experiment with different objects. He took the wheels off his brother's bicycle and put them on the back of his tricycle. He put the tricycle wheels on the bicycle. He liked being different. He always saw a new way to do things. *(You may want to use a personal story of someone you know in the place of this story.)*

Peter saw God's Spirit this way. Peter was a Jew, and the Jews had strict laws about what they could eat. Peter had a dream. A sheet came down from heaven. In the sheet were all kinds of animals the Jews believed they weren't supposed to eat. *(Let the children help you open the blanket/sheet with the various animals in it.)* A voice called out to Peter to kill an animal and eat it. Peter didn't want to do that. He thought it was wrong to eat those kinds of animals. The same thing happened again and again. The voice told him to eat—it was okay because God made it okay.

Right after his dream, men came to Peter to invite him to come to Caesarea. God's Spirit told Peter to go with them. There was a man in Caesarea named Cornelius. He had a dream that Peter could tell them how to be saved. As Peter began to speak about Jesus, God's Spirit, or what we call the Holy Spirit, came to all the people in the house. All the people in the house were Gentiles. People did not think of them as God's chosen people. Now Peter saw that God's Spirit could work in new ways. *(Open Bible.)* He said, *If then God gave them the same gift [of the Holy Spirit] that he gave us when we believed in the Lord Jesus Christ, who was I that I could hinder God?*

Sometimes we think God should do things our way. We sometimes forget that God can do anything. God's Spirit is here today. Talk with your family this week about what God's Spirit might do. Will we be ready to see how God's Spirit can create something wonderful that we could never do on our own? I hope you will talk about God's Spirit and how God's Spirit can help your family as you serve God this week.

What Makes Us Different?

Date: Fifth Sunday of Easter

Scripture: John 13:31-35

Key Verses: I give you a new commandment, that you love one another. Just as I have loved you, you also should love one another. By this everyone will know that you are my disciples, if you have love for one another. (John 13:34-35)

Key Concept: Love

Materials: Bible

I need helpers this morning. *(Choose children who will be able to tell the physical differences between themselves and another child, such as clothing, hair color, height, etc. If possible, try to choose children whose physical features differ greatly.)* Look at _____ and tell us how he/she looks different from you. *(Offer an example if necessary. Let the child respond.)* You saw many differences in each other.

When we look at each other, we can easily see differences. We have different hair colors, eye colors, and skin tones. We're different heights—some are short and some are taller. We wear different clothes. We have many differences. Jesus talked to his disciples about being different. *(Open Bible.)* In John 13, Jesus tells his disciples this: *I give you a new commandment, that you love one another. Just as I have loved you, you also should love one another. By this everyone will know that you are my disciples, if you have love for one another.* What did Jesus tell his disciples to do to show they were his disciples? How would other people describe them when they saw them? *(Let the children respond.)* That's right. Jesus told his disciples that if they loved one another, others who saw them would know they were his disciples.

The people sitting out there *(point to the congregation)* are what we call (name of church). A church is a group of people who gather to worship and serve Jesus together. A church is a group of people who are Jesus' disciples. We are taught to love one another so others will know we are Jesus' disciples. Can you think of ways we show love to one another? *(Let the children answer. Reflect back their answers.)* Let's all ask Jesus to help us love one another so others will see that we're Jesus' disciples.

Shine On Us

Date: Sixth Sunday of Easter

Scripture: Psalm 67

Key Verses: May God be gracious to us and bless us and make his face to shine upon us, that your way may be known upon the earth, your saving power among all nations. (Psalm 67:1-2)

Key Concept: God's presence/invocation

Materials: Bible

Preparation: This sermon might work best if used during the time of the invocation. Invite the children to the front right before you pray the invocation. Use the verses above as the prayer of invocation.

I'd like the children to join me up front for the prayer of invocation. *(Let the children come to the front and be seated. Included is a prayer of invocation. You may choose to write your own based on the verse from Psalm 67.)* Let's pray together. God, we pray that you will bless us, show us your grace, and shine on us, so that we can learn of your power and saving ways. Amen.

Every Sunday when we gather to worship, we say a prayer to begin our service. This opening prayer is called the invocation. In it, we ask God to be with us and help us worship. It helps us begin worship by thinking about God and praying together for God's help as we learn together.

In our prayer this morning, we asked God to shine on us. What do you think of when you hear the word *shine*? *(Let the children answer.)* Sometimes we think of the sun or a lamp that gives off light. Another way to think of shine is to stand out. If we put a light in a dark room, we can see the light. It stands out. In a way, we asked God to stand out so that we only think of God. We want God to be with us, and God is with us. We use the prayer of invocation to help us think only about God while we are here to worship God.

Is It Fair?

Date: *Sixth Sunday of Easter*

Scripture: *John 5:1-9*

Key Verses: *The sick man answered him, "Sir, I have no one to put me into the pool when the water is stirred up; and while I am making my way, someone else steps down ahead of me." (John 5:7)*

Key Concept: *Miracles*

Materials: *Bible, piece of paper, marker*

Preparation: *Prepare to play a game with the children. Choose children who volunteer to play. Use the questions listed below for the game. Have the children stand. Tell them to listen to the question. If they know the answers, they are to sit on the floor. Try to call on the child who sits first. Tell the children that the person who answers the most questions is the winner.*

Questions

(1) Name the mother of Jesus.

(2) Name one of Jesus' disciples.

(3) What job did Jesus' father Joseph have?

(4) Who built an ark because God told him to?

(5) In what town was Jesus born?

(6) Who helped God's people cross the Red Sea?

(7) Who was put in a cave with lions and protected by God?

(8) Who watched baby Moses while he floated in a basket in the river?

(9) Name the first book of the Bible.

(10) Who climbed a tree to see Jesus?

(11) Who baptized Jesus?

(12) Who helped God's people in the battle of Jericho where the wall came tumbling down?

(Explain the rules and play the game with the children. At the end of the game, declare a winner. Choose as the winner a child who didn't play. See how the children react and continue from that point.)

Were you surprised that _____ won the game, even though he/she didn't play? *(Let the children respond. They may complain that it is not fair.)* What does it mean to you for the game to be fair? *(Let the children respond.)*

(Open Bible.) In John 5, there's a story about Jesus that doesn't seem fair. Listen and see if you can figure out what isn't fair in this story. Jesus went to Jerusalem. In Jerusalem, there was a pool called Bethzatha. People who were sick would get in the water when it was stirred up, and they would be healed. One lame man sat by this pool for thirty-eight years. Jesus knew the man had been there a long time. He went to the man and asked him if he wanted to be made well. *The sick man answered him, "Sir, I have no one to put me into the pool when the water is stirred up; and while I am making my way, someone else steps down ahead of me."* The lame man didn't answer Jesus' question. He didn't ask how he could get well. All he could think of was the pool and how he never made it in time. Jesus healed him anyway.

Most of the people Jesus healed are those who went looking for him and had faith in him. They believed he was from God and could heal them. When Jesus healed people, he did a miracle. Jesus worked a miracle when he healed the lame man by the pool. This story shows that Jesus helps people who don't even ask for help. We don't have to do something for Jesus to work a miracle. We don't have to do something for Jesus to love us.

Sometimes, like in the game we played today, we expect to win because we got the most answers. We think that is fair. We want to make sure everyone plays the game by the rules. With Jesus, there are no rules about who Jesus loves or who Jesus helps. We don't have to do anything to receive the love of Jesus and the miracles that Jesus can do for us. That's different from the way we think sometimes, but I'm glad Jesus loves everyone and can work miracles in our lives even when we don't ask.

Call to Worship

Date: *Seventh Sunday of Easter*

Scripture: *Psalm 97*

Key Verse: *Rejoice in the Lord, O you righteous, and give thanks to his holy name! (Psalm 97:12)*

Key Concept: *Call to worship*

Materials: *Bible, church bulletins*

Preparation: *Have this children's sermon take place at the beginning of the service. Introduce the children to the call to worship.*

I brought everyone a bulletin. If you can read, you can follow along with the worship service. *(Give a bulletin to each child. If your church has bulletins prepared especially for children, use them.)* Let's try to learn this verse together. When we learn it, we will say it together as our call to worship with the rest of our church family.

The verse is from Psalm 97:12: *Rejoice in the Lord, O you righteous, and give thanks to his holy name.* Let's say it in smaller parts. *Rejoice in the Lord.* What does it mean to rejoice in the Lord? (Let the children respond.) It means we are joyful and glad to be in God's presence. We are ready to praise God. The next part of the verse is *O you righteous.* The word righteous describes you and me when we love God and act to please God. The last words of our verse are *and give thanks to his holy name.* This part of the verse tells us to give thanks to God while we worship.

Now let's say the call to worship together with our church family. We will say it slowly so everyone can follow along. *(If you have many little children, you might want to have them echo the verse in small parts the way it was broken up earlier. Lead the call to worship.)*

The verse we just said is the call to worship. The call to worship is part of our service every Sunday. Sometimes we say it together, or sometimes _____ leads us. The call to worship is like an invitation. You've received invitations to birthday parties. This is an invitation to worship God. It helps us begin to focus on why we have gathered in this place.

The call to worship is an invitation for everyone, including you, to come and worship God today. Let's worship God together.

Jesus Prayed for Us

Date: Seventh Sunday of Easter

Scripture: John 17:20-26

Key Verses: "I ask not only on behalf of these, but also on behalf of those who will believe in me through their word, that they may all be one." (John 17:20-21a)

Key Concept: Jesus' love

Materials: Bible

Preparation: Choose a sentence related to the sermon to use in the message game described below. An example is "Jesus prayed for us."

I need some volunteers. *(Choose up to twelve children depending on the size of your congregation and the number of children present. Also consider the children's ages. Assign each child a row of pews/chairs and have them tell the first person the message.)* Each of you is standing by a different row of seats/pews in the church. I want you to tell the message to the first person on the end of the row; then I want you to come sit down. *(To the congregation:)* I want the person on the end of the row to tell the message to the next person, and continue down the row in that way. Once you hear the message, please raise your hand. *(To the children:)* I want you to watch as the hands start going up in the air. See how fast the message spreads.

It looked like a wave as the message spread throughout the congregation. We shared this message: "Jesus prayed for us." Did you know that a long time ago, Jesus prayed for you and for all of us? *(Open Bible.)* In John 17:20-21a, Jesus says, *"I ask not only on behalf of these, but also on behalf of those who will believe in me through their word, that they may all be one."* It sounds like Jesus prayed for the disciples who were with him, but he also prayed for those who would believe because of the words they said.

The disciples began telling people. These people told other people, who told other people. It was like our message game. We watched as the message spread to all the people. The disciples began to spread the message of Jesus, and others have shared it year after year since Jesus was here on earth. In fact, for more than 2,000 years, the message of Jesus' love has been told. We're still telling it! We tell it each week. The message of Jesus will go on forever.

A Helper for Us

Date: Pentecost

Scripture: John 14:8-17

Key Verses: "If you love me, you will keep my commandments. And I will ask the Father, and he will give you another Advocate, to be with you forever." (John 14:15-16)

Key Concept: Holy Spirit

Materials: Bible

I will ask you a question, but don't answer out loud. You can nod or shake your head if you want to answer. When no one was watching, have you ever tried to get away with something? When your parents are in another room, have you tried to get by without washing your hands? Maybe you turned the water on so your parents would think you were cleaning your hands, but you didn't really wash them. Have you ever tried to get away without brushing your teeth? Maybe you even put toothpaste on your toothbrush, but when no one was watching you rinsed it off without putting it in your mouth.

When someone is watching us, we usually do what we're supposed to do. Sometimes, when no one is watching, it's easy to do enough to get by. Without someone there to watch us and help us, it can be easy to slip into sloppy habits. We can do what we are supposed to do, but we might not do it well or in the best way.

Jesus thought about his disciples often. He knew he would not be on earth with them much longer. He wondered what would happen to them after he left. How could they keep the commandments he taught them? He knew they faced a problem. When he was gone, they might fall back into the old way of life. But that's not what happened.

(Open Bible.) Jesus said to them, *"If you love me, you will keep my commandments. And I will ask the Father, and he will give you another Advocate, to be with you forever."* Another name for Advocate is Holy Spirit. The Holy Spirit would guide the disciples and help them keep Jesus' commandments.

Today, we celebrate the Holy Spirit coming to the church fifty days after the first Easter. We celebrate that the Holy Spirit can remind us, help us, and love us as we work or play each and every day.

Appendix

Comfort and Help

Date: Sixth Sunday in Lent (Palm Sunday—Years A, B, C)

Scripture: Isaiah 50:4-9a

Key Verse: It is the Lord God who helps me . . . . (Isaiah 50:9a)

Key Concept: God's comfort and help

Materials: Bible, teddy bear, self-adhesive bandages with key verse printed on them

I brought my favorite teddy bear today. Do you have a favorite stuffed toy you like to hold and cuddle? *(Let the children answer.)* When I was your age, I liked to play with my teddy bear when I was happy. I had tea parties and invited all the stuffed animals to come. Have you ever done that? *(Let the children respond.)* Sometimes when I was sad, it felt good to snuggle and hug my teddy bear. Have you ever felt sad and hugged your favorite toy? *(Let the children answer.)* Sometimes it's nice to have something to hug that comforts us—it makes us feel safe and cared for.

I also brought a box of bandages. Why do we need these? *(Let the children answer.)* We use bandages when we get cuts or scrapes. They keep dirt and germs from getting into the cut. They help us keep safe from dirt and germs that might make our cut worse.

On each bandage, I wrote a verse from Isaiah 50:9a. *(Open Bible.)* The verse says, *It is the LORD GOD who helps me.* It's good to know God helps us. Sometimes we have problems that are hard. We can't always fix our problems. The writer of this passage in Isaiah faced big trouble, but he knew God would help no matter what the problem was.

Jesus knew that, too. This week is what we call Holy Week. We will remember Jesus' last week on earth. During his last week, Jesus remembered that God helps. Jesus prayed and obeyed God. When trouble comes our way, we can remember that God helps and comforts us. We can pray and let God know our troubles because we know God always cares.

Branches and Light

Date: Sixth Sunday in Lent (Palm Sunday—A, B, C)

Scripture: Psalm 118:1-2, 19-27

Key Verses: The Lord is God, and he has given us light. Bind the festal procession with branches, up to the horns of the altar. You are my God. and I will give thanks to you; you are my God, I will extol you. O give thanks to the Lord, for he is good, for his steadfast love endures forever. (Psalm 118:27-29)

Key Concepts: God's power and goodness

Materials: Bible, palm branches, candles, matches, adult helpers

Preparation: Candles are optional. Consider using only the palm branches, or you could use electric candles. You might plan this activity for the beginning of the service and have the children prepare at the back and come forward for the children's sermon. End the children's sermon after the responsive reading. Print the words of the responsive reading in the bulletin so the congregation can participate.

I'm going to give you a palm branch or a candle for you to use this morning. *(Give out the items—candles for older children and palm branches for younger children, unless you have electric candles.)* I need everyone's attention. We're going to go to the back of the sanctuary and walk in with our candles and palm branches. Adult helpers will lead you in. Please follow them. As we walk down the aisle, other adult helpers will read a passage from Psalm 118.

Responsive Reading (Psalm 118:26-29)

Pastor/Leader: *Blessed is the one who comes in the name of the* LORD.

People: *We bless you from the house of the* LORD.

Pastor/Leader: *The* LORD *is God, and he has given us light.*

People: *Bind the festal procession with branches up to the horns of the altar.*

Pastor/Leader: *You are my God, and I will give thanks to you;*

People: *you are my God, I will extol you.*

Pastor/Leader: *O give thanks to the* LORD, *for he is good,*

All: *for his steadfast love endures forever.*

(Have the children sit for a moment and continue.) We just read part of Psalm 118. It tells us about God's power and goodness. Out of joy, we want to worship and give thanks. I want you to raise your hand if you are especially thankful to God for something today. When I call on you, I want you to say, "I am thankful to God for _____," and the congregation will say, "O give thanks to the Lord, for he is good, for his steadfast love endures forever." *(Let the children respond and then close.)*

This is our prayer today.

Shaped by Christ

Date: Sixth Sunday in Lent (Palm Sunday—A, B, C)

Scripture: Philippians 2:5-11

Key Verse: Let the same mind be in you that was in Christ Jesus . . . .
(Philippians 2:5)

Key Concept: Following Christ

Materials: Bible, chart paper, various shapes (heart, diamond, square, etc.),
cutout shape of human body, markers

I brought different shapes today. You probably know all these shapes, but I
want you to look at them with me. What shape is this? *(Hold up one of the
shapes and let the children answer. Continue with all the regular shapes.
Consider asking what items are like the shapes. For example, a diamond shape
looks like a kite.)*

What is this big shape? *(Hold up the human body shape and let the children respond.)* Yes, it's the shape of a person. Let's think about a special
person—Jesus. From the stories you have heard about Jesus, what was Jesus
like? When you tell me something about Jesus, I'm going to write it on the
body shape. *(Let the children respond. Assist with examples as necessary: kind,
loving, giving, helping, healing, etc. Write the children's answers on the body
shape.)*

These words describe what Jesus was like. As followers of Jesus, we
want to be like Jesus, too. *(Open Bible.)* Paul wrote in Philippians 2:5, *Let
the same mind be in you that was in Christ Jesus.* We are to be like Jesus. All
the words we used to describe Jesus should describe us, too.

As we get ready for Easter, try to be like Jesus. Pick one word that
describes Jesus and try hard to be like him in that way. If I choose the word
"helping," then I will try to help my family and friends in every way that I
can. Give it a try with your family. Ask God to help you be more like Jesus
every day.

Announcing the Good News

Date: Easter Sunday (A, B, C)

Scripture: John 20:1-18

Key Verse: Mary Magdalene went and announced to the disciples, "I have seen the Lord"; and she told them that he had said these things to her. (John 20:18)

Key Concept: Jesus' resurrection

Materials: Bible, person to do a monologue or puppet play depicting Mary Magdalene

Easter is the most important celebration in the life of the church. We get ready for Easter through special services, Bible readings, and prayer during Lent. Now it's here! Have you ever wondered what it was like to be there on the first Easter? I've thought about how the disciples and Mary must have felt to see Jesus killed on the cross. They must have been sad. It would have been a scary and confusing time.

Today we have a special guest from the past, Mary Magdalene. She will share about what happened on the first Easter. She was the first person to see that Jesus was alive. *(Open Bible.)* John 20:18 says, *Mary Magdalene went and announced to the disciples, "I have seen the Lord"; and she told them that he had said these things to her.*

(A puppet or a person in biblical costume can perform the following monologue.)

Mary Magdalene's Monologue

It was an amazing day. I got up early that morning and went to Jesus' tomb. When I came near, I could see that someone had moved the heavy stone! I was afraid. I ran back and found Peter and another disciple and told them the stone was gone. Jesus was gone, too. He was no longer in the tomb. I was upset, so I rested for a minute.

Peter and the other disciple ran as fast as they could to the tomb. Peter was slower, and the other disciple got there first. He told me he was too scared to go in without Peter, so he waited.

When I felt better, I went back to the tomb. Peter and the other disciple went inside. They believed me; they could see Jesus was not there. But they didn't understand what had happened. Neither did I. Peter and the other disciple went home.

I sat outside the tomb and cried. As I cried, I noticed someone in the tomb. Two angels were sitting where Jesus' body had been. They asked me why I was crying. I told them I couldn't help it. Someone had taken away my Lord. Then I saw another person behind me. It was Jesus! At first I didn't recognize him. I thought he was the gardener. I thought maybe he knew who had taken Jesus away. He asked me why I was crying and who I was looking for. I asked him if he knew where Jesus' body was taken. He called my name. He said, "MARY!" Right then I knew it was Jesus. I yelled, "TEACHER!" He told me to tell the disciples he was going to heaven to the Father. He told me to go and tell them I had seen him. I went and gave them the news from Jesus.

(At the end of the monologue, close with questions about the story, or sum-marize it and end with prayer.)

Rejoice!

Date: Easter Sunday (A, B, C)

Scripture: Psalm 118:1-2, 14-24

Key Verse: This is the day that the Lord has made; let us rejoice and be glad in it. (Psalm 118:24)

Key Concept: Rejoicing

Materials: Bible, children's instruments (optional), hymn: "This Is the Day"

Happy Easter! This is a very special day. This is the day when we celebrate Jesus' coming back to life. It's a day for rejoicing, which means we should be glad and happy.

The psalm writer knew about rejoicing. *(Open Bible.)* Psalm 118:24 says, *This is the day that the LORD has made; let us rejoice and be glad in it.* I brought rhythm instruments so we can make music. We will sing a song based on this verse. *(Have the congregation join you in singing the song, and have the children play along with the rhythm instruments.)*

How can we tell that others are rejoicing—that they're happy and glad today? *(Let the children answer. They may comment on flowers, special outfits, etc.)* We have so much to be happy about. Jesus has shown us how we are to live and love each other. That makes us glad. We have food, a home, friends, and family to celebrate this special day. That makes us glad. Most importantly, we are glad because Jesus is alive and is our Savior. I can tell you are happy and rejoicing by the smiles on your faces. May each of you have a happy Easter day!

Lord of All

Date: Easter Sunday (A, B, C)

Scripture: Acts 10:34-43

Key Verse: You know the message he sent to the people of Israel, preaching peace by Jesus Christ—he is Lord of all. (Acts 10:36)

Key Concept: Lord

Materials: Bible

Happy Easter! Today is a very special day of celebration. We celebrate that Jesus is Lord. In our Scripture reading from Acts 10, Peter gives a short version of this good news of Jesus. *(Open Bible.)* In verse 36, Peter writes, *You know the message he sent to the people of Israel, preaching peace by Jesus Christ—he is Lord of all.* Have you ever thought about why people called Jesus "Lord"?

In the Bible, the word "Lord" is used a lot. Lord can mean master or ruler. People who served someone or who were slaves called their masters Lord. Lord can be a title of respect or honor. When the centurion asked Jesus to heal his servant, he called Jesus "Lord." Jesus was called Lord as a respected teacher.

Have you ever seen the word "Lord" printed in capital letters in your Bible? This special name showed god was creator and ruler. The word "Lord" capitalized stood for the word "Yahweh." For God's people, Yahweh was God's name. It was too special to speak. They used "Lord" in place of it. This is another use of "Lord" in the Bible.

When we say Jesus is Lord, what do we mean? Sometimes we say Jesus is our honored teacher. Jesus has showed us how to live. Sometimes we call Jesus our master or ruler because we want to do what Jesus taught us. Most importantly, though, when we say Jesus is Lord, we say that Jesus was God as well as man. That is hard to understand, but it is true. It is part of what we call mystery, something we can't completely understand.

If we honor Jesus and let him be our master by doing what he taught us, then we live faithfully. We don't have to understand everything about Jesus to love and honor him. It's great to know and say, "Jesus is Lord."

Jesus' Words

Date: Ascension Sunday (A, B, C)

Scripture: Acts 1:1-11

Key Verses: "But you will receive power when the Holy Spirit has come upon you; and you will be my witnesses in Jerusalem, in all Judea and Samaria, and to the ends of the earth." When he had said this, as they were watching, he was lifted up, and a cloud took him out of their sight. (Acts 1:8-9)

Key Concept: Mission, ascension

Materials: Bible, magic trick materials (optional)

Preparation: If you or someone in your church is good at magic tricks, do something simple for the children to show that magic is only a trick. Explain how you perform the trick. If you choose this option, do the trick as the first part of the sermon and adapt as needed.

Today is Ascension Sunday. We read Scripture that tells about Jesus going up to heaven. The word *ascension* means to go up. *(Open Bible.)* Acts 1:9 says, *When he had said this, as they were watching, he was lifted up, and a cloud took him out of their sight.* Can you picture in your mind what the disciples saw when Jesus was taken to heaven? Can you picture Jesus rising up in the air until he was gone? *(Let the children respond if they wish.)* We might think of this as magic. It's not really magic, because magic is always a trick that your eyes don't see. The ascension of Jesus is what we call mystery. We can't explain how it happened, but we know the power of God made it happen.

More important are the words Jesus told the disciples before he went to heaven. We find them in verse 8: *"But you will receive power when the Holy Spirit has come upon you; and you will be my witnesses in Jerusalem, in all Judea and Samaria, and to the ends of the earth."* Jesus told the disciples they were to be witnesses. Witnesses are people who have seen something and can tell about it. The disciples saw and heard what Jesus said as he went around teaching, preaching, and healing. Jesus told them to do the same things he did. He promised to send the Holy Spirit to help them.

When we become Christians, we too are called to tell the story of Jesus to others. We can tell Jesus' story by the way we treat our friends, by the things we say, and by all the things we do. We could even rewrite this verse for where we live: "And you will be my witnesses in all of (your city/town), in all of (your country), and (country that your country doesn't particularly get along with), and even the rest of the world."

May each of us tell the story of Jesus.

Praying for Wisdom

Date: Ascension Sunday (A, B, C)

Scripture: Ephesians 1:15-23

Key Verse: I pray that the God of our Lord Jesus Christ, the Father of glory, may give you a spirit of wisdom and revelation as you come to know him. (Ephesians 1:17)

Key Concept: Wisdom/revelation

Materials: Bible, encyclopedia, dictionary, school books, computer disk, bag
Preparation: Place all the items in the bag.

I brought items in this bag. *(Take each item out of the bag as you explain it.)* Here's an encyclopedia. It is a book full of information about countries, animals, and people. We use an encyclopedia to learn things we don't know. Here is a dictionary. We use a dictionary to look up words to learn how to spell them and to find out what they mean. I also brought a schoolbook. It's a math book that helps us learn about numbers. Here is a computer disk that helps me learn about maps so I can find my way on a trip. We have so many ways of learning things we don't know.

When we learn new things and understand them, we say we have wisdom. I know _____ knows all about _____. *(Use this statement only if you know something about a child. For example, one of the children may know all about dinosaurs, weather, spiders, etc.)* We could say _____ has wisdom about _____. When _____ tells you about _____, (he/she) lets you see all there is to know about it. (He/She) gives what we call revelation—she/he shows or tells you so that you can understand all about something.

I have something else in my bag. *(Pull out the Bible.)* What does this book help me know? *(Let the children respond.)*

Paul prayed for wisdom and revelation for one of the churches he wrote. *(Open Bible.)* In Ephesians 1:17 he wrote, *I pray that the God of our Lord Jesus Christ, the Father of glory, may give you a spirit of wisdom and revelation as you come to know him.* Paul prayed that the people in this new church would know and understand Jesus more and more. There's always something new to learn about Jesus, and that was Paul's prayer.

What are some ways you can know more and more about Jesus? *(Let the children respond.)* There are many ways, such as reading the Bible, praying, learning from our Bible teacher, singing songs, and talking with our parents and friends. We have to want to know more about Jesus to get to know him more and more. *(You may want to lead into the next portion of the sermon by explaining baby dedication, depending on your tradition. Emphasize that parents have their children participate in these events as a way of promising to help children grow in the wisdom of knowing Jesus.)*

One of the reasons we gather each Sunday is because we want you to grow to know more and more about Jesus. We want you to know what it means to be a follower of Jesus so you can live in a way that pleases him. *(Lead the children in a prayer about growing in knowledge of Jesus so that they can show others his love.)*

The Pentecost Story

Date: Pentecost (A, B, C)

Scripture: Acts 2:1-21

Key Verse: All of them were filled with the Holy Spirit and began to speak in other languages, as the Spirit gave them ability. (Acts 2:4)

Key Concept: Pentecost

Materials: Bible

Today we celebrate Pentecost. I want to tell you about Pentecost so you can understand why we celebrate. God's people, the Israelites, celebrated three festivals every year. One of the festivals was called the Feast of Booths. It was a way to celebrate God's care for the people while they lived in the desert after leaving Egypt with Moses. Another festival was called the Feast of Unleavened Bread, which was a way to celebrate their freedom from slavery in Egypt. It included a Passover meal. Jesus' last supper with the disciples was the Passover meal. The third festival was called the Feast of Weeks, which was a time to thank God for the food they were able to grow. The name of this feast was changed to Pentecost because it was celebrated fifty days after the beginning of Passover. The word *Pentecost* means fiftieth.

God's people came to Jerusalem from all over to bring their harvest offerings to the temple. In Acts 2, we find the story of a special Pentecost when the Holy Spirit came. The Holy Spirit gave the disciples the ability to speak in other languages to tell the story of Jesus to all people. Jesus promised the disciples that the Holy Spirit would come to them, and it did on that day of Pentecost long ago.

(Open Bible.) Acts 2:4 says, *All of them were filled with the Holy Spirit and began to speak in other languages, as the Spirit gave them ability.* As the disciples began to tell the story and speak in other languages, the people were amazed. They couldn't believe what they heard. Peter stood up and spoke words from the Old Testament. He said God would pour out God's Spirit on all people. Peter continued to tell them about Jesus and how what the Old Testament prophets said came true in Jesus.

Today we celebrate the coming of the Holy Spirit to those who believe. Jesus promised to send the Holy Spirit to help us make choices and to teach us the ways that are pleasing to him.

Bibliography

Lord, Priscilla and Daniel Foley. *Easter the World Over.* New York: Chilton Book Co., 1971.

The New Oxford Annotated Bible. New Revised Standard Version. Edited by Bruce M. Metzger and Roland E. Murphy. New York: Oxford University Press, 1991.

Texts for Preaching: A Lectionary Commentary Based on the NRSV—Year A. Edited by Walter Brueggemann et al. Louisville: Westminster John Knox Press, 1995.

Texts for Preaching: A Lectionary Commentary Based on the NRSV—Year B. Edited by Walter Brueggemann et al. Louisville: Westminster John Knox Press, 1993.

Texts for Preaching: A Lectionary Commentary Based on the NRSV—Year C. Edited by Charles B. Cousar et al. Louisville: Westminster John Knox Press, 1994.

Scripture Index

Psalm 67	Sixth Sunday of Easter—C
Psalm 91	First Sunday in Lent—C
Psalm 97	Seventh Sunday of Easter—C
Psalm 98	Sixth Sunday of Easter—B
Psalm 107:1-3, 17-22	Fourth Sunday in Lent—B
Psalm 116:1-4, 12-19	Third Sunday of Easter—A
Psalm 118:1-2, 14-24	Easter Sunday—A, B, C
Psalm 118:1-2, 19-27	Sixth Sunday in Lent—A, B, C
Psalm 119:9-16	Fifth Sunday in Lent—B
Psalm 121	Second Sunday in Lent—A
Psalm 130	Fifth Sunday in Lent—A
Psalm 133	Second Sunday of Easter—B
Psalm 150	Second Sunday of Easter—C
Isaiah 43:16-21	Fifth Sunday in Lent—C
Isaiah 50:4-9a	Sixth Sunday in Lent—A, B, C
Isaiah 55:1-9	Third Sunday in Lent—C
Jeremiah 31:31-34	Fifth Sunday in Lent—B

New Testament Scripture Texts

Matthew 21:1-11	Sixth Sunday in Lent—A
Mark 11:1-11	Sixth Sunday in Lent—B
Luke 4:1-13	First Sunday in Lent—C
Luke 13:1-9	Third Sunday in Lent—C
Luke 15:1-3, 11b-32	Fourth Sunday in Lent—C
Luke 19:28-40	Sixth Sunday in Lent—C
Luke 24:13-35	Third Sunday of Easter—A
Luke 24:36-48	Third Sunday of Easter—B
John 2:13-22	Third Sunday of Lent—B
John 5:1-9	Sixth Sunday of Easter—C
John 11:1-45	Fifth Sunday in Lent—A
John 12:1-8	Fifth Sunday in Lent—C
John 13:31-35	Fifth Sunday of Easter—C
John 14:1-14	Fifth Sunday of Easter—A
John 14:8-17	Pentecost—C
John 15:1-8	Fifth Sunday of Easter—B
John 15:9-17	Sixth Sunday of Easter—B
John 17:1-11	Seventh Sunday of Easter—A
John 17:6-19	Seventh Sunday of Easter—B
John 17:20-26	Seventh Sunday of Easter—C
John 20:1-18	Easter—A, B, C
John 20:19-31	Second Sunday of Easter—B
John 21:1-19	Third Sunday of Easter—C

Subject Index

Faith/Love	Second Sunday of Easter—A
God's care/protection	Second Sunday in Lent—A
	Seventh Sunday of Easter—A
	Fourth Sunday of Easter—B
	First Sunday in Lent—C
God's comfort/help	Sixth Sunday in Lent—ABC
God's covenant	First Sunday in Lent—B
	Fifth Sunday in Lent—B
God's faithfulness	Second Sunday in Lent—B
God's inclusiveness	Fourth Sunday in Lent—C
God/Jesus' love	Third Sunday of Easter—B
	Seventh Sunday of Easter—C
God's power/goodness	Sixth Sunday in Lent—ABC
God's presence	Second Sunday of Easter—A
	Fifth Sunday of Easter—A
	Third Sunday in Lent—C
God's sovereignty	Third Sunday of Easter—A
God's Word/Truth	Third Sunday of Easter—A
	Fifth Sunday in Lent—B
	Second Sunday of Easter—B
	Seventh Sunday of Easter—B
	First Sunday in Lent—C
Grace	Fifth Sunday in Lent—C
Holy Spirit	Pentecost—A, B, C
	Fifth Sunday of Easter—C
Invocation	Sixth Sunday of Easter—C
Jesus as God's Son/Savior	Sixth Sunday in Lent—A
Jesus' humanity	Fifth Sunday in Lent—A
Jesus' identity	Third Sunday in Lent—B
	Third Sunday of Easter—C
Jesus as Lord	Easter—ABC
Jesus' resurrection	Easter—ABC
Judging	Fourth Sunday in Lent—A
Learning about Jesus	Third Sunday of Easter—B
Listening to God	First Sunday in Lent—A
Loving others	Fourth Sunday of Easter—B
	Fifth Sunday in Lent—C
	Fifth Sunday of Easter—C
Miracles	Sixth Sunday of Easter—C
Mission	Ascension—ABC
Palm Sunday	Sixth Sunday in Lent—B
Pentecost	Pentecost—ABC
Pleasing God/Jesus	Fourth Sunday in Lent—A

	First Sunday in Lent—B
	Third Sunday in Lent—B
Prayer	First Sunday in Lent—A
	Fifth Sunday of Easter—A
Proclaiming God/Jesus	Third Sunday in Lent—A
	Sixth Sunday of Easter—A
	Fourth Sunday in Lent—C
Rejoice	Easter—ABC
Reverence	Fifth Sunday in Lent—A
Salvation	Fourth Sunday in Lent—B
Sin/Forgiveness	Fourth Sunday of Easter—A
	Third Sunday in Lent—C
Thankfulness	Fourth Sunday in Lent—B
True happiness	Seventh Sunday of Easter—B
Trust	Second Sunday in Lent—A
	Third Sunday in Lent—A
	Second Sunday in Lent—C
	Fourth Sunday of Easter—C
Unity	Seventh Sunday of Easter—A
	Second Sunday of Easter—B
Wisdom/Revelation	Ascension—ABC
Witness	Easter—C
Worship/Praise	Second Sunday in Lent—B
	Fifth Sunday of Easter—B
	Sixth Sunday of Easter—B
	Sixth Sunday in Lent—C
	Second Sunday of Easter—C